THE DIME
DETECTIVES

THE DIME DETECTIVES

Ron Goulart

THE MYSTERIOUS PRESS

New York • London • Tokyo

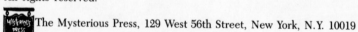The Mysterious Press, 129 West 56th Street, New York, N.Y. 10019

Printed in the United States of America

First Printing: December 1988

10 9 8 7 6 5 4 3 2 1

DIME DETECTIVE is a trademark of Argosy Communications Inc.

Library of Congress Cataloging-in-Publication Data

Goulart, Ron, 1933–
    The dime detectives.

    1. Detective and mystery stories, American—History and criticism. 2. American fiction—20th century—History and criticism. 3. Detectives in literature.
I. Title.
PS374.D4G68   1988   813'.0872'09   88-40074
ISBN 0-89296-191-0

I am indebted to the following people for providing me with information, advice, and dire warnings about what pitfalls to avoid: David Arends, Michael Barson, Carol Brenner, J. Randolph Cox, Walker Martin, Shirley Meech, Will Murray, William F. Nolan, Richard Sale, Robert Sampson, Henry Steeger, James L. Traylor, Robert Weinberg, and Martin Wolson.

Your private detective does not want to be an erudite solver of riddles in the Sherlock Holmes manner; he wants to be a hard and shifty fellow, able to take care of himself in any situation, able to get the best of anybody he comes in contact with, whether criminal, innocent by-stander or client.

—Dashiell Hammett

CONTENTS

Chapter 1

The Dime Detectives

The hard-boiled private eye, tough, cynical, and yet often sentimental, made his initial appearance as a fully evolved character in the 1920s. He first showed up in the untrimmed pages of the pulpwood fiction magazines, but within a decade he was to be found between the covers of hardbound books issued by respectable publishers, on movie screens across the nation, and even in the funny papers. He eventually became a popular entertainment stereotype—along with the cowboy, the gangster, and the jungle man—and made his way into every medium. This book deals with roughly thirty years of his life, concentrating on his career in the pulps. This opening chapter focuses on the pulp magazines themselves, what they were and what they had to offer, and the various events and characters contributing to the advent of the modern private investigator as a literary type.

One such character was newspaper and magazine publisher Frank A. Munsey, a man not universally admired. When he expired in 1925, he was even attacked in some of his obituary notices. "Frank Munsey contributed to the journalism of his day," said one, "the talent of a meat packer, the morals of a money changer and the manner of an undertaker." Be that as it may, Munsey was the father of the pulp magazine, and had it not been for him there might never have been a Tarzan, Sam Spade, Doc Savage, Zorro, or Shadow. Zane Grey might have remained a dentist and Charles Atlas a ninety-seven-pound weakling.

A telegraph operator in his hometown of Augusta, Maine, Munsey left there for New York in 1882, when he was in his late twenties. He wanted to publish a cheap fiction weekly of inspirational stories for children. The *Golden Argosy* was launched as a weekly magazine at the end of 1882 and included fiction by Horatio Alger and Edward S. Ellis, a noted writer of dime novels. At this point Munsey was in competition with a great many other better-established publishers. Weekly story papers had been available for almost a half century. "Popular literature on the scale marketed today is as much a product of the Industrial Revolution as is large-scale manufacture of any sort," points out historian Mary Noel. By Munsey's day the printing and distribution of the fiction papers had vastly improved over what it had been at the start. He also had to worry about competition from dime novels, begun original-ly as spin-offs of the literary newspapers but soon turned into a major genre of their own. Beadle & Adams got into the dime novel trade during the Civil War. In 1889, while Frank Munsey was still floundering and was more than $20,000 in debt, Street & Smith started a dime novel line. It had been in the fiction weekly business since the 1850s and soon discovered that the five- and ten-cent novels could be equally profitable.

Munsey was having what one biographer described as a time that was "financially fruitless." He kept modifying his shaky publication. He trimmed the title down to *Argosy* and aimed it at older juveniles and adults instead of children. In 1891 he started another magazine, entitled *Munsey's*. This low-priced, illustrated, general audience magazine did well, providing him with both money and inspiration. Munsey decided to gain for *Argosy* the kind of general adult audience *Munsey's* was enjoying. And at the same time he had an idea how to save some money: cheaper paper.

"Tinkering with *Argosy*," says *Magazines in the Twentieth Century*, "he made it an all-fiction magazine and switched to rough wood-pulp paper because he thought the story was more important than what it was printed on. Publishers of cheap fiction may have seen that the pulp could save postage. As single publications, dime novels were not eligible for the low second-class postage rates; the pulp magazine was."

Munsey's new package of mass fiction was a fat pulp-paper magazine with no pictures, and the public soon decided it liked this format. *Argosy's* circulation quickly climbed to 80,000 an issue and by the early 1900s was selling a half million copies a month. During the first dozen successful years of his two magazines, Munsey not only got free of debt but he earned himself a net profit of $9 million. During World War I, by which time he'd added *All-Story* and *Cavalier* to his pulp titles, he made *Argosy* a weekly again. Until the Munsey Company introduced *Detective Fiction Weekly* in the 1920s, all its pulp fiction publications were broadly general. Every story category that would eventually have a pulp of its own appeared, including romance, science fiction, western, and detective.

Street & Smith followed Munsey into the pulps. It started *Popular Magazine* in 1903, first as a juvenile and then as an imitation of *Argosy*. *Top-Notch*, another all-category fiction magazine, followed in 1910. Then Street & Smith got the notion that there might be money in specializing, and the result was *Detective Story*, *Western Story*, *Love Story*, *Sea Stories*, and *Sport Story*. When this last title showed up in 1923, the dime novels were long gone and the pulp magazine was the dominant format for adventure and romantic fiction. At the close of World War I barely two dozen different pulp titles were on sale, but by the middle of the Depression there were several hundred. Such long-established publishers as Doubleday and the Butterick Company also started publishing cheap fiction magazines. Doubleday took over *Short Stories* in 1910 and later added both a cowboy and a mystery adventure one. Butterick's chief pulp was *Adventure*. Brand-new people set up shop, too, and contributed to the proliferation of titles in the years between the wars.

A standard pulp magazine format had been arrived at by the twenties, and most of the houses conformed to it. The average pulp consisted of from 112 to 144 pages and had a cover of more expensive coated stock. The cover served as both package and advertisement, so it had to be bright and provocative. Basic colors and intense action prevailed. Prices ranged from five cents to twenty-five cents, with fifteen cents the average price in the twenties. The Depression, as we'll see, brought a wave of dime magazines.

Pulp magazines grossed millions and publishers were

fond of them, but they had few champions in critical circles. The detective pulps weren't considered any different from the other denizens of the cheap paper ghetto. Typical of the critical attitude are the remarks on the pulps in an article by one Margaret MacMullen in the July 1937 issue of *Harper's*. "It is not pleasant to think of the immature minds and mature appetites that feed on such as their staple fodder, but there is no ducking the fact that sensationalism is the age-old need of the uneducated," she laments. "The steady reader of this kind of fiction is interested in and stirred by the same things that would interest and stir a savage."

Miss MacMullen comes to this conclusion after quoting several pulp detective stories, all of which sound like the work of Robert Leslie Bellem, a prolific writer whom we'll be encountering in later chapters. Writing in the *Saturday Review of Literature* at just about the same time, Fletcher Pratt observed that "most pulp stories have no plot; merely proceed from the original *données* through situation after situation till the author allows one of these to crystalize out into a solution of his contracted wordage."

It was Pratt's theory that "Conan Doyle is the ancestor of shoals of detective pulps." Since "Doyle never allowed Holmes to be funny . . . to this day there is a taboo on humor among detective magazines." The fact that Pratt himself had been contributing to the science fiction pulps since the late 1920s, something not mentioned in his article, may have clouded his feelings about the entire pulpwood business.

Cheap, popular fiction has been deplored ever since it struggled into existence in the nineteenth century. Some concerned critics and commentators in every era have been fearful the stuff would corrupt youth. Every mass-media hero from Deadwood Dick and Frank Merriwell to Super-man and Spider-Man has been viewed with alarm. Often, too, though not openly stated, a class element is involved, a resentment on the part of some that the peasants have been allowed to learn to read at all. Detective fiction was criticized from the outset, but the volume of criticism was proportionate to the amount of detective stories available.

Detectives were not abundant as fictional heroes until relatively late in the nineteenth century. Edgar Allan Poe's tales of Dupin's adventures in crime appeared in 1841 but did not herald a trend. The detective novels of Emile Gaboriau, written in the 1860s, were widely pirated in America, as were those of Charles Dickens and Wilkie Collins. *Bleak House*, published in 1852, briefly features Inspector Bucket, possibly the first detective to appear in British fiction. Collins's books, such as *The Moonstone*, in 1868, also make use of professional detectives.

The activities and memoirs of Allan Pinkerton and the private-detective agency he founded in 1850 were also influences on the development of cheap fiction detective stories in the United States. Pinkerton eventually gathered some of his cases together, and his casebook was issued with the Pinkerton slogan "We Never Sleep" and his wide-open eye trademark on the cover. Other casebooks fol-lowed. By the 1880s the story paper publishers were issuing libraries about a number of detectives and inves-tigators: Old Cap Collier, Old Broadbrim, Dick Dobbs, Old King Brady, Young King Brady, and Old Sleuth. Old Sleuth had first appeared in the *New York Fireside Companion* in 1872. The *Old Sleuth Library*, a monthly dime-novel series, started in 1885. Old Sleuth shared this one with a variety of other detectives. "The prevailing theme throughout the *Old Sleuth Library* is the concept of the Great Detective (a different one in each number) whose 'wonderful exploits and hair-breadth escapes . . . are all described in brilliant style,'" explains J. Randolph Cox in *Mystery, Detective and Espionage Magazines*. "There is a Lightning Detective, a River Detective, a Ventriloquist Detective, a French Detective, a St. Louis Detective, an Irish Detective, a Yankee Detective, several other ethnic detectives, and three women detectives. The most delightfully named of the latter is Lady Kate, the Dashing Female Detective." Mary Noel attributes the increasing popularity of Old Sleuth and similar detectives as much to an urban setting for the stories as to their plots: "The detective was perfectly adapted to the confused traffic and bewildering ways of the rapidly growing city."

Sigmund A. Lavine, in his biography of Pinkerton, contends that

> as more and more publicity was given to Pinkerton's National Detective Agency, publisher George P. Munro conceived the idea of using its founder as the central character in a series of stories crammed with violent action and filled with continuous suspense, in which evil was always punished. No dime novels were ever more successful than these yarns about "Old Sleuth" which were inspired by Pinkerton's skill as a detective. "Sleuth," incidentally, is an old Scotch word for the trail left by a man or beast and it, too, has passed into American-English as a synonym for detective. Actually, it was extremely

difficult to make the fictional "Old Sleuth" as clever, colorful or competent as Allan Pinkerton. Fond of disguising himself, he maintained a large collection of costumes and wigs.

This is the place to lay to rest the notion that Pinkerton's wide-eyed logo gave the private eye his name. This foolishness has turned up in several histories, and a recent one expresses it thus: "The term 'private eye' dates back to the mid-nineteenth century when the detective agency founded by Allan Pinkerton used a wide-open eye and the slogan 'We Never Sleep' as its trademark." The actual explanation can be found in most any dictionary. The one I use says that the eye in private eye is a "phonetic rendering of I, abbr. for investigator."

One of the hardiest of nineteenth-century detectives was Nick Carter, a Street & Smith product. He made his bow in a cameo part in their *New York Weekly* in 1886 in a yarn entitled "The Old Detective's Pupil; or, The Mysterious Crime of Madison Square." He was soon promoted to a series of his own. Like Frank Merriwell, Nick Carter was clean-cut and impressively strong. Though he did a sufficient amount of clue-gathering and trail-following, he appealed to boy readers not as much for his ratiocination as for his derring-do. He could box, fence, swim, and operate whatever new mechanism came along—automobile, airplane, etc. And, as the logo on the 1890s' *Nick Carter Weekly* indicated, he was a master at appearing in various disguises. There is an air of unreality, of melodramatic hokum about the adventures, and Nick Carter, as J. Randolph Cox notes, "has been referred to as one of the blandest heroes in detective fiction." Cox adds that "he is a mythical figure representing the flawless mastery of good triumphing over evil while hiding his identity behind a series of disguises." There was, however, an effort made to involve Nick with real locales and even some of the real criminals of the day. "He could, and did," says Cox, "go everywhere to solve mysteries; out West chasing the Daltons, to Chinatown rooting out opium dens, to London or Paris tracking international crooks." Even when in the great open spaces tangling with the Daltons Nick didn't neglect his disguises: "In this story he not only appears in his own person, but as various members of the Dalton Gang (he nearly fools one of the Daltons himself), a Jewish shopkeeper, and a Bowery hoodlum."

Detectives appeared in just about all of the general fiction pulpwoods, like *Argosy*, *Adventure*, and *Blue Book*. Many were of the Nick Carter design, but there were also cerebral sleuths, such as Jacques Futrelle's Thinking Machine, and a whole string of scientific investigators. Detective short stories were very popular from the 1890s onward, due initially to the impact of Sherlock Holmes, and were also staples of the slick-paper magazines. A misconception about the genre is that this type of material was shunned by the more respectable, family-oriented periodicals. One misinformed scholar, in summing up the first two decades of the twentieth century, says, "it was essentially low-brow entertainment, and while an occasional mystery made its way into the pages of the slick paper magazines, stories about crime and criminals were largely confined to the pulps, those cheap, lurid publications sold at newsstands." On the contrary, detective tales were frequently seen in all the major slicks and had been throughout the period. The Sherlock Holmes stories, with

Frederick Dorr Steele's impressive illustrations, were very popular in *Collier's*, and Conan Doyle's detective was often depicted on the weekly's covers from 1903 onward. In the 1920s Holmes appeared in both *Liberty* and Hearst's *International*. The rivals of Sherlock Holmes were also much in evidence in the pages of the slicks in the early decades.

R. Austin Freeman's Dr. Thorndyke, his methodical investigations illustrated by Steele, was to be found in *McClure's*. E. W. Hornung's stories about the Crime Doctor, illustrated by Steele, ran in *Everybody's*. Among the other detectives who showed up on high-class paper were Mr. Tutt, Uncle Abner, Charlie Chan, Philo Gubb, and several created by E. Phillips Oppenheim. Frederick Irving Anderson was a frequent contributor to *The Saturday Evening Post*, and readers of *Collier's* could follow Nayland Smith's never-ending conflict with the insidious Dr. Fu Manchu.

When the initial pulp detective magazines arrived, what they offered was not something rarely to be found elsewhere but rather more of the same and in larger quantities. There were, as we'll see, few differences in what the two kinds of publications, pulps and slicks, offered in the early days.

Chapter 2

Nick Carter Strikes Again

Appropriately enough, the first pulpwood magazine devoted exclusively to detective fiction was edited by none other than Nick Carter himself. Or so Street & Smith would have had the readers of the early numbers of *Detective Story* believe. The first issue carried the date October 5, 1915, on its bright red cover, and sold for ten cents. Before the pulps faded away some forty years later, over two hundred other detective fiction pulps would be printed. A multitude of sleuths, ranging from Sam Spade to the Shadow, would come to life on their untrimmed pages. But Nicholas Carter and his cohorts quite likely didn't anticipate any of that.

Actually the new twice-a-month pulp rose from the ashes of an earlier S&S publication. *Nick Carter Stories*, the third of the nickel weeklies devoted to the formidable investigator, had first appeared in 1912. By the time the cheap paper 32-page weekly was nearing its 160th issue in 1915, the feeling around the office was somewhat less than enthusiastic. "Youngsters are getting tired of reading about the same characters week after week," Ormond Smith is alleged to have said to his brother William. "They're getting fed up with Nick Carter." These feelings had been inspired by Street & Smith Vice-President Henry W. Ralston, who was anxious to launch a detective fiction pulp and had been pitching the idea to his superiors. Ormond liked the notion and told Ralston and his brother Will, according to Quentin Reynolds's official history of the firm, "Let's discontinue the *Nick Carter Weekly* [*sic*] and start a magazine that will have a dozen different detectives as characters. Perhaps some of them will catch on. We'll call it—Oh—Let's see . . . What do you think of *Detective Story*, Will?"

The final issue of the older magazine, dated October 2, 1915, broke the news in an "Announcement Extraordinary":

> *Nick Carter Stories* has outgrown its present form and we are going to publish it in magazine style. It will be edited by Nicholas Carter, and will be called *Detective Story*. It will be published on the fifth and twentieth of each month, and will contain, besides a rattling good serial, telling of the exploits of Nick Carter, serials and short stories dealing with the detective art in all its forms.

The Nick Carter serial, *The Yellow Label; or, The Drive Against Crime*, was carried over from the weekly to the new pulp. "Thus, Nick Carter entered the pulp era after 24 years," leading Carter historian and researcher J. Randolph Cox has observed.

Reynolds contends in *The Fiction Factory* that S&S intended the new periodical to be "aimed at youngsters as well as adults who enjoyed stories of murder and larceny." One wonders how many adults actually believed that Nicholas Carter was sitting behind the editor's desk. The man really to be found there was Frank E. Blackwell, a young reporter from the *New York Sun*, who'd recently been hired by Ralston. In addition to the second installment of *The Yellow Label*—"From the archives of Nicholas Carter"—and a brief Headquarters Chat with Nick, Blackwell offered readers of that first issue five short stories, a novelet, and an episode of another serial. None of those long-ago writers featured in the issue—such as Ross Beechman, Arnold Duncan, and R. Norman Grisewood—managed to earn lasting reputations in the mystery field.

Although Street & Smith may have believed the public was growing a mite weary of Nick Carter, that didn't prevent them from seeing to it that all sorts of Nick Carter surrogates appeared in *Detective Story* during its first few years. Among these were Pinklin West, Kingdon Cole, and the redoubtable Thorndyke Flint. Credited to the house penname of Douglas Grey, the Flint yarns were so close to those of the master that, as Cox has discovered, some of them "were later revised as bonafide Nick Carter stories for Street & Smith's papercovered novel series." Like his model, Flint was a "famous criminal investigator, whose reputation as a solver of inscrutable mysteries was as wide overseas as in his own country." Seen by the world as a "well-built, steady-eyed man in an unobtrusive business suit," Flint could be galvanized by as little as a whiff of a clue, at which times he "dropped his rather nonchalant manner and was as tense and alert as a crouching jaguar."

Flint's was the world of private clubs and the right sort of people, and he succeeded chiefly because the clients, criminals, and minions of the law that he encountered were even less bright than he.

For the most part the private-detective stories of this period seemed to be cast in the past. In a gaslit Victorian world where vast conspiracies were hatched in secret lairs, keen investigators and criminal masterminds alike were masters of disguise and, often, the methods and motives of both crooks and detectives had little to do with reality. Whatever the operatives called themselves, they were usually imitators of either Sherlock Holmes or Nick Carter. This was true of the majority of private investigators doing business in *Detective Story* in the teens and, for that matter, throughout most of the twenties. They were, like the earlier real-life detectives—Allan Pinkerton and William J. Burns—who'd given their memoirs to the world, squarely on the side of the established system. None was a maverick or a cynic.

Detective Story did make room for a few misfits, but they were all crooks and scoundrels. These included a variety of masked and mysterious rogues, like the Gray Phantom and Black Star, who we'll take a closer look at in a later chapter. Con men and crooks were represented by such as Amos Clackworthy, Simon Trapp, and Boston Betty. The prolific Johnston McCulley contributed a great many humorous stories about a lisping pickpocket known as Thubway Tham.

Detective Story caught on. Commencing with the September 4, 1917, issue, it became a weekly and it continued as one until the early 1930s. Thereafter it returned to its twice-a-month schedule. The success of Street & Smith's pioneering mystery pulp did not, however, start a land-slide. During the ten years after its launching, only four other detective fiction magazines came into being.

The first competitor arrived in the autumn of 1917, a slim, 64-page periodical called *Mystery Magazine*, published, every other week more or less, and selling for a dime. The magazine, according to pulp historian Sam Moskowitz, "carried over many dime novel authors as contributors" and was edited by Luis P. Senarens, the creator of the Frank Reade stories—("Frank Reade and his Steam Man," etc.). Most of the early stories, reports Robert Sampson in *Mystery, Detective and Espionage Magazines*, "feature improbable policemen and crooks . . . none of them seeming competent to cross the street without being run over by a circus parade." Things perked up a bit in the mid-1920s when writers like Frederick C. Davis, Agatha Christie, and Charles G. Booth appeared in the magazine's pages. While not exactly thriving, *Mystery* managed to hang on, suffering various price, size, and format changes, until 1929.

Much more formidable competition for *Detective Story* was *The Black Mask*, a pulp that first appeared in 1920 and would eventually change the mystery field for good and all. Its long, influential career will be covered in the next chapter.

The Munsey folks got into the field in the summer of 1924 with a weekly that was initially titled *Flynn's* and offered nearly 200 pages of short stories, novelets, and serials for ten cents. By 1928 the pulp was called *Detective Fiction Weekly* and as such it lasted until the early 1940s.

The ostensible editor of the new Munsey weekly was a thickset man with a prominent undershot jaw. His name was William J. Flynn and he was the former chief of the United States Secret Service. Working on *Flynn's* and gaining many new friends through its pages was, he told his readers, a thrill to him, especially since this was a "project involving a man's hobby as well as his life work." No stranger to the writing of detective fiction, Flynn had collaborated on a series that ran in *Argosy* in 1922. The stories dealt with the exploits of "Peabody Smith, the famous investigator, late of the United States Secret Service, and now retired after years of fine service." They are bland, firmly in the Nick Carter camp, and give little evidence of being written by anyone with firsthand knowledge of crime and its detection. For the readers of *Flynn's* he produced nonfiction, his memoirs in six parts. "All my life I have been a detective," begins *My Life in the Secret Service.* "That must be my excuse for writing the story of my life for this magazine."

In the fiction department, Flynn gathered together a variety of detectives. These included Ernest Bramah's blind investigator, Max Carrados; Inspector Malcome Steele, of the National Detective Agency; a magician detective known as the Great Mandell; and Anthony Wynne's Dr. Hailey—basically a blend of American and British operatives. An extra element of mystery showed up in the introduction to a serial by Homer Eon Flint. "In death the author of 'The Money-Miler' has delved into as great a mystery as fiction ever knew," wrote the editor. "A month or two ago the body of Homer Eon Flint was discovered lying at the bottom of a lonely fifty foot cañon near San Jose, California, pinned beneath the ruins of a wrecked taxicab. On their arrival the police found no clews pointing to the presence of any other human being on the spot at the time the mysterious tragedy took place."

Probably the most famous detective to be found in *Flynn's* at this period was Arthur B. Reeve's Craig Kennedy. The scientific detective had been around since 1910, showing up in such magazines as *Cosmopolitan*, *Adventure*, and *Detective Story*. Kennedy was, as the *Encyclopedia of Mystery and Detection* puts it:

> a chemist who uses his knowledge to solve cases. He is also one of the first detectives to use psychoanalytic techniques. He is a professor at Columbia University but also earns fees for his work as a consulting detective. A man of action as well as thought, he is a master of disguise and often uses a gun when circumstances require it.

Reeve's sleuth started appearing in hardcover books in 1912. In the teens and twenties his books had a large following in this country and he is said to have been the largest-selling American mystery writer in England at that time. Just before World War I Craig Kennedy moved to the silver screen in a sequence of serials, with scripts Reeve worked on, that starred Pearl White and an actor named Arnold Daly. These included *The Exploits of Elaine*, *The New Exploits of Elaine*, and *The Romance of Elaine*. A fringe benefit of these chapter plays was the introduction of such memorable villains as the Clutching Hand and the insidious Wu Fang.

Reeve was not an impressive author, despite his popular success, and the Kennedy stories have not survived the test of time. In *Yesterday's Faces* Robert Sampson comments, "What we have, then, is the standard mixture of astute private investigator, complete with stooges, who performs his marvels supported by the usual amiable officials. All this is written in a prose from which most sensory cues have been stripped, after which each sentence has been ironed flat." For *Flynn's*, Reeve produced several groups of Kennedy yarns. The initial batch had the overall title *Craig Kennedy and the Elements* and included stories entitled "Air," "Fire," and "Water." Next came points of the compass ("North," "South," etc.) and then one using the senses ("Sight," "Smell," etc.). In the mid-1920s Reeve was a pudgy, balding man in his middle forties who nonetheless posed for a magazine cover photo impersonating his detective.

The fourth magazine to emerge during the decade after the advent of *Detective Story* was *Detective Tales*. First seen in the autumn of 1922, the pulp issued from the same publisher as *Weird Tales*. Vincent Starrett, Seabury Quinn, R. T. M. Scott, and Arthur J. Burks were among the contributors. "The stories emphasized amateur investigators of remarkable mental abilities," observes Robert Sampson, "and adventures among gangsters of the Prohibition era. The action was brisk, the scene contemporary." The magazine folded in the early 1930s, but the title came back from a different publisher.

No new detective pulps were introduced in 1925. The only one to emerge in 1926 was *Clues*, a product of the W. M. Clayton house. Before its collapse during the early years of the Depression, the company was responsible for such titles as *Ranch Romances*, *Ace-High*, and *Astounding Stories*. The early contributors to *Clues* were a mixed lot that included Carolyn Wells, Erle Stanley Gardner, who appeared frequently from the second issue on, H. Bedford Jones, Oscar Schisgall, and Lemuel DeBra ("he was with the U.S. Secret Service about thirteen years, you will remember").

By the late 1920s the popular arts had discovered organized crime. The advent of Prohibition nearly a decade earlier had brought everyday citizens and crooks closer together by way of speakeasies and bootleggers. Gangsters, gamblers and gunmolls became acceptable dramatic characters; tommy guns, tuxedos and slick black touring cars graced movie screens and magazine covers. Josef von Sternberg made *Underworld* in 1927 and *The Dragnet* in 1928; Frank Capra directed a gangster film called *The Way of the Strong* in 1928. From 1927 through 1929 nearly a dozen and a half new crime and detective pulps hit the stands. These included *All Star Detective Stories*, *Best Detective*, and, more significantly, *The Underworld*, *The Dragnet*, *Racketeer Stories*, and *Gangster Stories*.

Most of these latter pulps were originally dedicated to glorifying the American hood. They were considerably more hard-boiled in approach than the other detective pulps noted thus far in this chapter. They met with little success, though, and with considerable opposition from civic groups dedicated to cleaning up the newsstands of the nation. Another wave of gangster pulps came along in the 1930s, but, as Will Murray points out, "the later versions . . . featured stories where the gangsters usually met with bad ends in the individual stories. This was not always the case in the earlier magazines, and this was what the public most objected to." *The Dragnet* managed to hold on, thanks to an overhaul by A. A. Wyn, who bought the faltering pulp from Harold B. Hersey and changed its name to *Detective-Dragnet*. In 1933 the pulp changed again, this time into *Ten Detective Aces*.

Although the twenties was a transition period, it was not the heyday of the hard-boiled private eye. Almost none of the crime and mystery pulps that followed in the wake of *Detective Story* were aware that a revolution was under way. They were content with the more sedate sort of private investigator, with Nick Carter surrogates and genteel imports from Great Britain. But in the thirties nearly 140 more detective pulps came into being, almost every one showing the influence of the one magazine that had pioneered in the twenties with stories of a new sort of private eye. That magazine was, of course, *Black Mask*.

Chapter 3

The Black Mask School

The papers are either roasting me for shooting down some minor criminals or praising me for gunning out the big shots. But when you're hunting the top guy, you have to kick aside—or shoot aside—the gunmen he hires. You can't make hamburger without grinding up a little meat.
—Race Williams

Don't be too hard on him. Being around movies all the time has poisoned his idea of what sounds plausible.
—The Continental Op

Toward the end of his life, Joseph T. Shaw, former army captain and then literary agent, began to put together an anthology of detective stories. Though he eventually sold the book, entitled *The Hard-boiled Omnibus*, Shaw had a difficult time with it. This was in 1946 and there wasn't much interest in that first postwar year in the dead-and-gone period when Shaw had been editor of a pulp magazine called *The Black Mask*. He persisted, believing that something important had happened in the decade he'd been with the magazine. He didn't claim credit for what had happened, but Shaw was pleased to have been around when it did.

During the years 1926 to 1936 the hard-boiled detective

story had grown up and been perfected in the pages of *Black Mask*. It was during these years that Dashiell Hammett's *Red Harvest, The Glass Key,* and *The Maltese Falcon* ran as serials there. Raymond Chandler's first stories were published in this same span of years. Also appearing were Erle Stanley Gardner, George Harmon Coxe, Horace McCoy, Raoul Whitfield, Norbert Davis, and Lester Dent. And it was in these years and in this magazine that the private eye became an important American hero.

The private eye could only have happened in those years after World War I, the years of Prohibition. There had always been aggressive, straight-shooting fiction heroes, but it took the mood of the twenties to add cynicism, detachment, a kind of guarded romanticism, and a compulsion toward action. The disillusionment that followed the war and frustration over the mushrooming gangster control of the cities affected the detective story as much as they did mainstream fiction. The same things that were bothering the heroes of Hemingway, Dos Passos, and Fitzgerald began to unsettle the private detectives. And the 1920s' preoccupation with the American language, the dissatisfaction with Victorian rhetoric and polite exposition, was nowhere more strongly felt than among the writers of pulp detective fiction.

Though few critics have admitted them to the club, most of the *Black Mask* pioneers were also members of the Lost Generation. Hammett, for example, was born in 1894, the same year as E. E. Cummings, Laurence Stallings, and Donald Ogden Stewart. Among the authors born between 1885 and 1905 were Edna St. Vincent Millay, Ben Hecht, Dorothy Parker, Edmund Wilson, John Dos Passos, F. Scott Fitzgerald, Robert E. Sherwood, William Faulkner, Ernest Hemingway, Malcolm Cowley, Raymond Chandler,

Raoul Whitfield, Carroll John Daly, Erle Stanley Gardner, Frederick Nebel, and W. T. Ballard.

The new private detectives of the pulps, though varied individuals, shared certain attitudes and qualifications. They usually stayed away from small towns, most of them working for detective agencies in the large cities—New York, Chicago, San Francisco, Detroit, Los Angeles. They shared a distrust of politicians and the police. They could patiently collect evidence, but they could also cut corners the way the law couldn't. Yet they were linked with reality, with the real crimes of the urban world and the real smell and feel of the mean streets, and this put the best of them in a different class from the essentially adolescent phantom avengers and the earlier dime-novel sleuths with their upper-class values and methods. They were sometimes drunk, frequently broke. A private eye would always help someone in trouble, though he would downplay his compassion: "I could have walked away. I started to walk away and then the sucker instinct got the best of me and I went back." Taking action was what was important, even when it wasn't well thought out. Though the operative wasn't always an optimist, he stuck to his word: "It wasn't worth it, but then it was a deal."

The Black Mask was started because H. L. Mencken needed money. Man of letters and professional curmudgeon, Mencken and his literary accomplice, theater critic George Jean Nathan, had become coeditors and co-owners of *The Smart Set* during World War I. Subtitled "A Magazine of Cleverness," *The Smart Set* printed what the partners considered quality fiction and articles and was usually in shaky financial shape. Early in 1919 Mencken wrote to his friend Ernest Boyd, "I am thinking of venturing into a new cheap magazine scheme, and if I do it will tie me to New York all summer. The opportunity is good and I need the money."

Mencken and Nathan had already been involved with a couple of other pulps. These were *Saucy Stories* and *Parisienne*, both of which drew on the *Smart Set* slush pile for their material. After turning down the opportunity to do an all-Negro pulp, Mencken and Nathan finally decided they'd do a mystery magazine. By this time Street & Smith's *Detective Story* had proven a success.

Mencken christened the new thriller *The Black Mask*. The name may have come to him while looking at the cover of *The Smart Set*, which each month featured a line drawing of a black-masked Satan in its left-hand corner. *The Black Mask* made its debut early in 1920. By April, sales were looking good, though Mencken detested his magazine. "Our new louse, the *Black Mask*, seems to be a success," he remarked in a letter. "The thing has burdened both Nathan and me with disagreeable work."

Actually most of the early work seems to have been handled by Wyndham Martyn and Florence Osborne, associate editors of *The Smart Set*. The early issues of *The Black Mask* also made use of rejects from the other publications. Mencken and Nathan never allowed their names to appear on their new louse, and Miss Osborne, under the more masculine-sounding name of F. M. Osborne, was listed as its first editor. As the magazine's circulation climbed, Mencken grew no fonder of it. "*The Black Mask* is a lousy magazine—all detective stories," he complained. "I hear that Woodrow reads it. Reading mss. for it is a fearful job, but it has kept us alive during a very bad period."

While the magazine was still quite young, Mencken and Nathan sold it—the price has been reported as everywhere from $12,000 to $100,000. They'd started it with a cash outlay of $500, so no matter what the price, there was a considerable profit. One of their partners in *The Smart Set*, Eltinge Warner, became the owner and publisher of *Black Mask*. Warner, who had made a hit of *Field & Stream*, remained with *Black Mask* until 1940. Like Mencken, he thought little of detective stories, and the writer he liked least was Dashiell Hammett.

Although one of Mencken's favorite topics, in both *The Smart Set* and, later, *The American Mercury*, was the American language, *Black Mask's* early stories reflect little awareness of how America was talking as the 1920s commenced. A typical story began:

> When Mr. George Mitchell propped the *News* against the sugar bowl and dug into his matutinal grapefruit, he was unused to interruptions by persons answering classified advertisements; but on this particular morning, the maid casually remarked that there was some one at the door inquiring for a position as chauffeur.

And dialogue exchanges such as this were still going on:

> "Well," he observed, "it's certainly an odd thing that Sir Cheville Stanbury should come to a violent end immediately after making a will in which he left a pretty considerable sum of money to a young woman on whom his own solicitor was evidently far gone, isn't it?"

"What's to be done?" asked Marston. "Are you going to tell the police?"

"That's precisely what we don't intend! No, sir, Sir Marston, what we know or think we'll keep to ourselves for awhile! Don't say a word of what we may be thinking to a soul—not even to your mother."

As William F. Nolan points out in *The Black Mask Boys*:

[the] writers supplied pale imitations of the fiction being printed in *Detective Story*. Early *Black Mask* crime solvers were dull and pretentious fellows, reflecting the overbaked melodramatic elements of the silent screen. They included foppish Inspector Des Moines, prim and proper Desmond Okewood, of the British Secret Service, and solemnly pompous criminal investigator F. Jackson Melville-Smith. Bores one and all. . . . The awkward, heavy-handed titles of these early stories were in keeping with their outrageous plots and characters: "The Deviltry of Dr. Waugh," "The Strange Case of Nathaniel Broome," "The Uncanny Voice," "The House of the Fiend Who Laughs," "The Scar of the Gibbering Imp."

But while Sir Marston fretted over what to tell his mother and Mr. George Mitchell pushed aside his matutinal grapefruit, the real world began to invade *Black Mask*. Prohibition had happened, and detective stories that talked about hip flasks, homemade gin, and gangsters started appearing alongside the more polite tales of the upper classes and English gardens. Gradually, too, *Black Mask* began to attract writers who were trying, sometimes clumsily, not only to deal with homemade problems but to write in the American style and achieve a vernacular.

Out in suburban White Plains, New York, a mild mustached young man started talking tough:

> Now, when I say I'm an honest man I mean I'm honest to a certain extent. When I deal with an honest man I play him honest and when I deal with a crook I play him—I play him at his own game.
>
> You see crooks is my meat. They're simple, almost childish and what makes them easy picking is that they lack a sense of humor.
>
> And now for how I came to have Ed, the Killer, on my tail and gunning for me night and day.

This is Carrol John Daly, early in 1923, a few months after he started selling to *Black Mask*. What Daly was trying to do was come up with a tough private operative who narrates his own adventures. Daly, a former movie projectionist and theater manager, had good intentions, but he suffered from a tin ear. He undoubtedly soaked up too much bad silent movie melodrama as well. Even so, Daly invented one of the first of the new type of private eye. The earliest name he gave to his detective was Terry Mack— Three Gun Terry Mack, to be exact. He showed up in the May 15, 1923, issue. The very next issue, that of June 1, was *Black Mask's* special Ku Klux Klan number. Therein Daly introduced Race Williams, who was destined to become the most popular hard-boiled detective of the twenties. The issue was intended to build circulation and editor George Sutton proclaimed it "the most interesting and sensational number of any American magazine this year." It was devoted entirely to stories dealing with the KKK. Other contributors included Herman Pettersen, Robert L. Heiser, and Ray Cummings, who provided a humorous tale entitled "T. McGuirk—Klansman." In the opinion of E.R. Hagemann, "*Mask* claimed absolute neutrality toward the Klan, but it had difficulty hiding its tacit support and encouragement." Daly's story was called "Knights of the Open Palm" and opened:

> Race Williams, Private Investigator, that's what the gilt letters spell across the door of my office. It don't mean nothing, but the police have been looking me over so much lately that I really need a place to receive them. You see, I don't want them coming to my home; not that I'm particular, but a fellow must draw the line somewheres.
>
> As for my business, I'm what you might call a middleman—just a halfway house between the dicks and the crooks. Oh, there ain't no doubt that both the cops and the crooks take me for a gun, but I ain't—not rightly speaking. I do a little honest shooting once in a while—just in the way of business. But my conscience is clear; I never bumped off a guy what didn't need it. And I can put it over the crooks every time—why I know more about crooks than what they know about themselves. Yep, Race Williams, Private Investigator, that's me.

Reminiscing some two decades later, Daly claimed that he'd gotten Race into the magazine on a fluke. George Sutton was editor by 1923 and while he was off on vacation,

> Harry North, who later was to shape the destiny of *Black Mask*, was associate editor. . . . Harry bought two Race Williams stories, hustling me along on the second one.
>
> The editor, George Sutton, returned and I heard nothing from *Black Mask* for about four months. It was after both of the stories had been printed that George Sutton called me in. The nature of our talk, or rather his talk, was how bad he thought my Race Williams was. He didn't like the stories. He didn't like the characters. . . . Then he said:
>
> "It's like this, Daly. I am editor of this magazine to see it make money. To see the circulation go up. I don't like these stories—but the readers do. I have never received so many letters about a single character before. Write them. I don't like them. But I'll buy them and I'll print them. If you do bad work you will be the one to suffer. You can make money with this boy Williams, every one seems to like him but me."

Race Williams kept right on being popular. His name, usually in red letters, on a *Black Mask* cover was good for a 15 percent jump in circulation. Race was a tough, straight-shooting, wise-talking pragmatic urban cowboy. He was cynical, didn't trust anyone. Yet he could be sentimental over a girl in trouble. There were no neat timetable crimes in his world. Mostly he fought against gangsters, crooked politicians, and the occasional criminal mastermind Daly couldn't refrain from tossing in. Race couldn't get along with the police and they were edgy about him, continually warning him not to be so relentless in his gunning down of crooks and suspects. "Right and wrong are not written statutes to me," explained the detective, "nor do I find my code of morals in the essays of long-winded professors. My ethics are my own. I'm not saying they're good and I'm not admitting they're bad, and what's more I'm not interested in the opinions of others on the subject." He arranged things so his idea of justice always triumphed. Most problems can be solved by action: "It's not what you should have done that counts in life," he said. "It's what you do."

The world Race Williams operated in was a sort of nightmare projection of the real world of the twenties and thirties. It was a night world, filled with speakeasies, gambling joints, penthouses, run-down hotels. Hoods kept their hat brims pulled low, packed .45s in the armpit, drove long black cars. There was no safety. The people Race was trying to help were continually being shot at, kidnaped, tortured. Sometimes he'd have to rescue the same woman over and over again. Despite the dangers and the unpredictability of life, Race Williams made sure he kept himself in control. "I don't allow the unexpected to happen," he explained, "if I can prevent it."

Like many private detectives who followed, Race was impatient and aggressive. In his over three decades in the trade he kicked down innumerable doors, pushed aside countless bodyguards to get to the boss. He also enjoyed shooting:

I squeezed lead and the show was over. No hero holding his chest and giving a last message to his surviving countrymen. He was dead five times before he hit the floor.

I just raised my left hand and tightened my finger. He was leaning over, almost above me, when I let him have it. Nothing artistic about my shooting then. There wasn't meant to be. . . . Hulbert Cloverly dropped the knife from his left hand and clutched at his stomach. He screamed too—cursed once, and raised his right hand. But he didn't fire again. I don't know if he had the will or the nerve, or even the strength to—but I do know he didn't have the chance to.

Race had the habit of turning to the reader on occasion and justifying all this killing:

I closed my finger on the trigger and shot the gunman smack through the side of the head. Hard? Cold-blooded? Little respect for life? Maybe. But after all, it didn't seem to me to be the time to argue the point with the would-be killer.

There were times when Race Williams didn't even have to do any shooting. He simply flashed his guns:

I leaned slightly forward so for a moment he got a flash of two guns—one under each arm. . . . I said simply, "When you put Race Williams out of a rat trap like this, you'll have to put him out in a cloud of smoke."

The word "simple" appears often in the Carroll John Daly stories and serials: "In that second I let him have it. Simple? Of course it was simple." To Race there was no problem that couldn't be cleared up by simple, active means. In his adventures, as an ad put it, you found "no long explanations, no discussions of evidence." Daly, working quietly in White Plains, had invented a fictional type who fit in with the temperament of the years between the wars.

He has been for most historians and critics of the hard-boiled detective field a somewhat embarrassing founding father. He's a key figure, the creator of an important character, but he was not a very good writer and, for a man said to have a sense of humor, he seemed completely unaware of how silly both he and Race Williams sometimes sounded. Professor Philip Durham described him as "a careless writer and a muddy thinker" while crediting him with creating "the hard-boiled detective, the prototype for numberless writers to follow." Michael Barson, in *Clues: A Journal of Detection*, summed him up as "a third-rate word-spinner who hatched a second-rate protagonist who did his thing in these third-rate productions." In *The American Private Eye* David Geherin points out that "Daly never developed as a writer," but he acknowledges that "it was Race Williams who was the first to deliver a telling blow to the priggish intellectual sleuths like Philo Vance who dominated mystery fiction in the 1920s."

Erle Stanley Gardner, looking back on his pulp days, said that Race Williams "was, perhaps, the forerunner of all the hard-boiled detective characters." He felt that Daly had done as much as any writer to develop that type of story and that he "started his stories with action and told them in terms of action." Gardner couldn't refrain from saying, in a 1965 piece in the *Atlantic Monthly*, that "Carroll John Daly had never had the slightest experience with actual crime or criminals, much less with bullet wounds." He went on to say:

> Daly himself wanted no part of the rough and tumble. When winter came, he shut himself up in a house which was regulated by thermostatic control, so the temperature never varied over two degrees one way or the other. . . . It was Daly's habit to sleep until noon. He would then get up and spend the afternoon in carefree ease with the family or with any other visitors who dropped in. After the family had been safely tucked in bed and the visitors had gone home, Daly would come to life. He would sit at his typewriter and pound out words until five or six o'clock in the morning. During those early hours the incomparably hard-boiled, bone-crushing, fast-shooting Race Williams came to life.

The intensity of Daly's writing and his long loyalty to his detective may have an obvious explanation. In an interview with James Traylor, Daly's daughter-in-law suggested that

> When he was drunk, he was Race Williams. He went into that alter ego. The rest of the time he was Caspar Milquetoast. . . . When he got drunk it was serious. That's when he was Race. That's when my husband and his friend Al would have to go from bar to bar looking for "Race."

They all knew Race because he would leave a trail behind him. All the bartenders called him Race.

Fortunately for the future and long-range survival of the private eye, Dashiell Hammett appeared at the same time as Daly. And to Hammett the world was anything but simple. "I drank a lot in those days," he later recalled, "partly because I was confused by the fact that people's feelings and talk and actions didn't have much to do with one another." The private eye that Hammett created for *Black Mask* in the early 1920s was much different from Race Williams, a more complex and more subtly handled figure. He had none of the swagger or the flash of Daly's hero. He didn't even have a name. He worked as an operative for the Continental Detective Agency in San Francisco and his first-person adventures were recounted in a terse, detached style.

The Continental Op, as Hammett's new detective came to be called, never bragged about his prowess with his fists or guns. He showed you, usually downplaying his ability. After shooting the gun out of a man's hand, for instance, the Op added, "It looks like a great stunt, but it's a thing that happens now and then. A man who is a fair shot (and that is exactly what I am—no more, no less), naturally and automatically shoots pretty close to the spot upon which his eyes are focused." The police didn't look on him as a crazed vigilante. They knew he was a competent professional, a man with several years' experience in the slow, patient business of being an investigator, and they cooperated with him on most cases.

The first Contential Op story, "Arson Plus," was printed in the October 1, 1923, issue. Commenting on it, William Nolan says:

In that one the Op described him as "a busy, middle-age detective" more interested in solving the crime than in "feminine beauty." From the outset he was anti-women when it came to a case; the Op was all business. When he talked to a woman, "I discarded the trick stuff—and came out cold-turkey." He'd been with the Continental of San Francisco for "four or five years" and was "an old hand at ducking bullets and reading truth behind lies."

Using a restrained vernacular style, and using the foggy San Francisco of the twenties as a setting, Hammett went on to write a series of stories about the Op, stories with real people, real motives, and real murders. Unlike most of his contemporaries in the crime pulps, Hammett had been a private detective himself. He had worked several years for the Pinkerton Agency, joining up in his hometown of Baltimore just before World War I. By the mid-twenties he quit for good. "I was getting sour on being a detective," he said. "The excitement was no longer there."

Hammett was married now, living in San Francisco and suffering from tuberculosis. He took a job writing copy in the advertising department of a Market Street jeweler. Explains Nolan:

Hammett wanted to record his unique experiences on paper, but fiction was a trade he knew nothing about. So he drank, trying to "figure things." Alcohol and lack of sleep underminded his health, and Hammett's lungs gave way. . . . Ignoring his wife's pleas, Hammett refused hospitalization. They argued. He left his family (by now they had a two-year-old daughter) and rented a cheap hotel room in downtown San Francisco.

Hammett made his earliest sales to Bill Kofoed's *Brief Stories*, a pulp devoted to the short-short. Apparently he aimed next at *Smart Set*, but missed and hit *Black Mask*. That resulted in the Continental Op's being born.

The short, heavyset Op was both sardonic and sentimental. He, too, would shoot a man if he had to and help a girl who needed protecting. He was quiet about it all, though. When a client becomes overly dramatic in explaining a problem, the Op tells him, "What's the use of getting poetic about it? If you've got an honest job to be done, and want to pay an honest price for it, maybe I'll take it." Despite the fact that he sometimes got involved with sinister Orientals, family curses, and religious cults, Hammett's operative has a fairly realistic conception of detective work. "Ninety-nine percent of detective work," he said, "is a patient collecting of details."

The Op drinks, smokes Fatima cigarettes, but when he is on a case he doesn't get involved with women. When he did feel strongly about a young woman, the Op would talk himself and the girl out of it: "Well, good God, sister! I'm only a hired man with a hired man's interest in your troubles." Hammett did romanticize the profession in at least one way. As a Pinkerton he'd had to work as a strikebreaker on the side of the moneyed interests, but the Op was allowed to have more scruples and never had to club a picket.

In 1929, in a *Black Mask* serial, Hammett introduced another private detective: Samuel Spade, who undertook the hunt for the Maltese Falcon. Spade was a little less detached than the Op, a little less restrained. He had been sleeping with his partner's wife and he was not reluctant about doing the same thing with female clients. Still he had his code, and when his partner was killed, he set out to avenge him. Spade didn't get along with the law as well as the Op, since he always put his own interests ahead of theirs. But he was about as honest as a man can be in the complicated world he had to function in. Hammett detached himself a bit more from the Spade adventures by writing in the third person, but he did give Sam Spade the first name he himself had abandoned when he began writing. *The Maltese Falcon* introduced a few more of the standard private-eye props, particularly the loyal young woman secretary who guards the outer office. *The Maltese Falcon* was issued in book form in 1930 by Knopf. In 1931 came the first movie version, from Warner Brothers, with Ricardo Cortez as Spade and Una Merkel as his secretary, Effie. Sam Spade would be much more influential on the pulp detectives of the thirties than the Op.

When Joseph Thompson Shaw took over as editor of *Black Mask* in 1926, he was in his early fifties and had lived a life that mixed writing and adventure. He'd attended Bowdoin College, where he edited the campus newspaper, worked on a New York daily, been on the staff of a trade journal, been a master swordsman, traveled in Spain, and served as a bayonet instructor in World War I. His army rank of captain stuck with him for the rest of his life, most of his contributors calling him Cap Shaw. He'd gone to *Black Mask* initially to try to sell stories, but got taken on as editor instead. When he was given the editorship of the magazine, he had never actually read a copy of it, or any other pulp magazine. Of the writers previous editors had introduced and encouraged, Shaw singled out Hammett as the one to be the cornerstone of his version of *Black Mask*. "Hammett was the leader in the thought that finally brought the magazine its distinctive form," he said later. "Without that it was and would still have been just another magazine. . . . Hammett began to set character before situation, and led some others along that path."

Shaw was to see the magazine through some very important years. He was there for the dying days of the Jazz Age, for the trauma that followed the stock market crash, and for the increasing bleakness of the Depression. The violence of organized crime, symbolized in the public mind by such events as the St. Valentine's Day Massacre of 1929, found its way more and more into the pages of *Black Mask*. As did the awareness of the political corruption that Prohibition and the get-rich-quick attitudes of the twenties had encouraged.

By 1926 several of the magazine's major writers had already appeared there. In addition to Hammett and Daly there were Raoul Whitfield, Frederick Nebel, and Erle Stanley Gardner. Gardner had first hit the magazine in 1924. It had not been easy for the Southern California attorney to break in:

> I kept hammering away at the *Black Mask* market. . . . Every now and then I sold a story. Sutton ceased to be editor. Phil Cody became editor, and Phil Cody heartily disliked my style of writing. But Phil Cody had an assistant editor by the name of Harry North, who was a patient cuss with something of a sense of humor, and Harry

wasted his time with me, giving me a little coaching on the margin of rejection slips and in short personal letters. . . . I began to write better stories and then *Black Mask* bought one. But I still couldn't plot worth a darn.

Among his first series characters was Bob Larkin, an adventurer who used a billiard cue as a weapon.

The billiard-cue cane, by the way, may need a little explainin'. For fifteen years, startin' as a boy, I've been a juggler, and a good one, too. I'm the one who originated the act of sittin' down at a table and startin' throwing plates around, mixing in the cups, and keepin' 'em all in the air at once. I never pack a gun. I don't need to. A gun makes people suspicious, and gets you into all kinds o' trouble. Nope, just give me a billiard-cue cane, and I'm all set.

There were also Ed Jenkins, a sort of rogue private eye who hid out in San Francisco's Chinatown and was known as the Phantom Crook, and Black Barr, a cowboy. Throughout the twenties *Black Mask* ran some western and adventure yarns along with the detective stuff.

Although Gardner sold over sixty stories to Shaw, he was apparently resentful of him. In the 1930s some of his earliest Perry Mason novels were said by reviewers to be imitation Hammett. In defending himself Gardner responded, "Hammett is not entitled to be given exclusive use of anything which he did not discover. . . . Jack London wrote stories of grim conflict before Hammett was ever heard of." According to Dorothy B. Hughes in her biography of Gardner, he believed that the success of *The Maltese Falcon* had "turned Cap Shaw into such a worshipper of Hammett that he tried to have all his authors write like him. Gardner felt that he himself was slighted in the magazine because only those authors who *would* imitate Hammett received first class treatment."

When Shaw came to put together his *Hardboiled Omnibus* in 1946, he tried to include one of Gardner's Ed Jenkins stories, "The Heavenly Rat," but Gardner flatly refused. He said, "Of late I have had a very strong feeling that my best work or even my typical work was not in *Black Mask* and I don't think it would do any good to have some of that work published side by side with the work of writers who were doing their best work in the magazine." He also informed Shaw that "Phil Cody is a friend of mine. Frankly I am getting damn sick of the attitude on the part of your friends to belittle Cody's part in *Black Mask*. . . . I wrote you dozens of times that your attempt to make the style . . . uniform would put *Black Mask* into the red ink. It did." Actually, as William F. Nolan demonstrates in *The Black Mask Boys*, Shaw boosted the circulation for the magazine during the first nine of his ten years there: "When Shaw had taken over in 1926, he increased circulation from 66,000 to 80,000 in the first year. The climb continued, peaking in 1930 to 103,000—but by the close of 1935, as America was suffering through the Depression era, circulation slumped to 63,000." Shaw it was who serialized not only *The Maltese Falcon* but *Red Harvest*, *The Dain Curse*, and *The Glass Key* as well. He also bought Paul Cain's grim, laconic Los Angeles crime novel *Fast One*. And an impressive number of writers first appeared in *Black Mask* during his stay. These included Horace McCoy, Norbert Davis, Theodore Tinsley, Roger Torrey, H. H. Stinson, W. T. Ballard, Raymond Chandler, George Harmon Coxe, John K. Butler, and Lester Dent.

Two of the writers who did the most toward developing the hard-boiled private eye after Hammett were Nebel and Whitfield. Although both had started appearing in *Black Mask* early in 1926, neither got around to creating a full-fledged tough P.I. until the autumn of 1930. That was, probably significantly, just about a year after the advent of Sam Spade. Whitfield's Ben Jardinn, who seems to be the very first Hollywood private eye, we'll discuss in our chapter on the West Coast branch of the profession. The character that Nebel came up with was Donahue—"an iron-nerved private dick," a blurb called him—who first showed up in the November 1930 issue. This is the same issue in which the final Continental Op story, "Death and Company," appeared, and it also included the final episode of Whitfield's *Death in a Bowl.* "Shaw wanted more Sam Spade stories, but Hammett refused to provide them," says William F. Nolan. "He was earning big money in Hollywood and had quit the pulps. Shaw asked Nebel to come up with a new private eye directly in the Spade mold, a series character he could feature in *Mask.* Nebel obliged with ultratough 'Donny' Donahue, of the Inter-State Detective Agency in New York, an ex-cop discharged from the force because he wouldn't bend to local corruption." The Donahue stories, like the Sam Spade novel, are written in the third person and appear to be exploring the approaches used by Hammett.

Nebel, however, once told me that, although he was a friend of both Hammett's and Whitfield's, "we never read one another's published work." He added, "We spent a lot of time together socially and I don't recall that we ever talked about Shaw's influence as an editor. We were too busy clowning around in bars to talk shop." As for the Spade novel,

> I did read *The Maltese Falcon*, but that was about a year after it had appeared in book form. Hammett and I got stoned one night and I woke up the next morning with an autographed copy. The inscription reads: "To Fred Nebel, in memory of the night of the cloud-burst when we were companions under the umbrella." This referred to a cloudless, starlit night when we strode up Lexington from 37th Street to Grand Central Terminal under an open umbrella, checked the umbrella (insisting that it remain open) and went into the Oyster Bar for some kind of shell food. We returned to the apartment in 37th with the umbrella still open. The idea seemed to be (there was a small bet) that no one would pay any attention to us. No one did.

Nebel concluded, "Since we were not influenced by each other's work I can only surmise that we reflected the times we lived in. . . . For my own part I know that Shaw never told me how to write for him, or what to write, nor did he ever ask for a revision or make one himself."

There were fifteen Donahue stories in all, the last of which appeared in the March 1935 issue. Donahue is tough and has a pragmatic sense of justice. He can be sentimental, but his usual attitude is one of slightly weary cynicism.

He accepts his world and his job and doesn't have any crusader's illusions that he can change things. About his profession he feels that it's a way to make a living but "no guy ever wrote a poem about it." There is considerable violence in the Donahue stories and Nebel describes it the way he describes the other elements of his environment. Getting shot at and beaten up is a part of Donahue's life, just as are the shadowy speakeasies, the sweltering summer streets, and the slick hoods. "Nebel is not a sensationalist," says David Geherin in *The American Private Eye*, "relying on gratuitous descriptions of graphic violence to add excitement to his tales; rather he uses violence to bring out the physical durability of his hero, a durability paid for by his suffering. Nebel's point is not that Donahue is immune to pain and suffering but that he is tough enough to endure whatever demands his dangerous profession makes of him." Nebel's other important private eye was Jack Cardigan. Similar to Donahue, but much more rumpled and considerably more outspoken, Cardigan hung out in *Dime Detective* and we'll meet him there in the next chapter.

Tough detectives of all sorts were on the *Black Mask* payroll in the Depression years. In addition to Ben Jardinn, Whitfield wrote of Ben Carey, Don Burney, Don Free, and Dion Davies. Under the pen name Ramon Decolta he produced two dozen stories about Jo Gar, the little Manila-based detective. Gar was tough, but in a quiet, self-effacing way. Ellery Queen once described the Jo Gar stories as having "the best features of the hard-boiled manner: the aura of authenticity, the staccato speech, the restrained realism. The tales are lean and hard—and unforgettable." Whitfield knew his locales firsthand, having been "to Guam, Manila, and Japan at the age of eighteen."

Of all of Shaw's *Black Mask* writers who experimented with different ways to tell a hard-boiled story, none came up with a more impressive variation than J. J. des Ormeaux—the pen name hiding a gentleman named Forrest Rosaire. He did three stories in rapid-fire first-person present. They were "Murderer's Night" (April 1930), "The Cross by Ximado" (February 1932), and "The Devil Suit" (July 1932). The last two feature Jack McGuire, a U.S. government investigator, and they are not quite like anything else before or since. There's action, humor, violence, and a sort of wild appreciation of the sheer wackiness of life. "The Devil Suit" begins:

> This is one night up in L.A. when Steve Parker and I are driving home after a little game with the boys. Out on Los Feliz Boulevard Steve sees the sign of Barr's Café and pulls up to the curb, saying, "How's for a steak?"
>
> "Sure thing," I says.
>
> As soon as Steve opens the café door we're greeted by an uproar. Sounds like most of the occupants are throwing pots and pans at each other, but we finally make out it's all coming from one booth down the line where we see an occasional arm or leg or ketchup-bottle leap forth. The rest of the customers are looking kind of apprehensive; the help has a pale pinched look around the gills.

The des Ormeaux style was good for depicting violence, as in this brawl scene from "The Cross by Ximado":

With that I get my feet on Vane's chest and heave from the shoulders. The big boy starts a parabola and comes down on one elbow and part of Shelly. It's time enough for me to roll to the gun and get to my knees when Vane comes up.

Shelly's not very big. Vane takes him off like he'd take off a coat. Then he comes for me again.

I'm set to sock him with the gun and I do, right in the middle of the face where the teeth show. He fumbles around at this, starts to sit down, and as he does Shelly pops him from behind.

It's a dumb thing to do; I don't know whether it hits him or not; he turns around in a slow surprised fashion with his knees still bent and says:

"Why, you little puking——!"

He simply reaches for Shelly, picks him up like a mother would a baby, and starts to throw him out the window.

In 1933 a forty-five-year-old businessman who'd been hurt by the Depression decided to see if he could write the kind of private-eye stories he'd been enjoying in the pulps. It took Raymond Chandler five months to turn out his first story, "Blackmailers Don't Shoot." Shaw bought it for *Black Mask* and Chandler gave himself over to writing pulp novelets. Though educated in England, he was fascinated with the American language. To speak, to write in a truly American style was important to him and had been since he was a young man. He later said:

I was distinctly not a clever young man. Nor was I at all a happy young man. I had very little money,

although there was a great deal of it in my family.
I had grown up in England and all my relatives
were either English or Colonial. And yet I was
not English. I had no feeling of identity with the
United States, and yet I resented the kind of
ignorant and snobbish criticism of Americans that
was current at the time. During my time in Paris
I had run across a good many Americans and most
of them seemed to have a lot of bounce and
liveliness and to be thoroughly enjoying themselves in situations where the average Eng-
lishman in the same class would be stuffy or
completely bored. But I wasn't one of them. I
didn't even speak their language. I was, in effect,
a man "without a country."

By the early 1930s Chandler was living in Southern
California. He'd found his country and could speak its
language and was on his way to finding Philip Marlowe.
"Although Philip Marlowe was not introduced by name
until 1939, he had been developing in Chandler's short
stories for a half dozen years," points out Philip Durham in
an essay on the Black Mask School.

Chandler's original private eye, using the name
Mallory, appeared in *Black Mask* in December
1933. From that date through 1939, he performed
in twenty short stories, usually as a private
eye. . . . He used ten different names and was
twice nameless, but always a part of the man
Marlowe was to become. In experimenting with
viewpoint Chandler used the first person twelve

times and the third person eight. Once created Marlowe was always a first-person narrator; this technique kept him on the scene, involved in the lives of others.

The first-person private investigator Chandler was developing, no matter what name he appeared under, always talked in a controlled, vernacular, and, at the same time, poetic style:

Carolina Street was away off at the edge of the little beach town. The end of it ran into a disused interurban right of way, beyond which stretched a waste of Japanese truck farms. There were just two houses in the last block, so I hid behind the first, which was on the corner, with a weedy grass plot and a high dusty red and yellow lantana fighting with a honeysuckle vine against the front wall.

Chandler's detective was a dedicated man, an honest man. He wasn't in it just for the money. Usually he was driven by a stubborn sense of justice. He got along with the police if they were straight. If they were crooked or on the take, he had contempt for them. Most of the stories were set in Southern California, a shabby wonderland that Chandler loved to explore and expose. His private eye always operated out of a small run-down office and lived in a small run-down apartment.

Raymond Chandler was fully aware of what he was up to, of what he was attempting with the private-eye story and what his detective stood for. Of his hero he said, "He is a failure and he knows it. He is a failure because he hasn't any money. . . . But he is a creature of fantasy. He is in a false position because I put him there. . . . Your private detective in real life is usually either an ex-policeman with a lot of hard practical experience and the brains of a turtle or else a shabby hack who runs around trying to find out where people have moved to." Of his general purpose in writing about private detectives Chandler summed up, "It is not a very fragrant world you live in, and certain writers with tough minds and a cool spirit of detachment can make very interesting and even amusing patterns of it."

Somewhat surprisingly, Chandler and Erle Stanley Gardner were pen pals. In a 1939 letter to Gardner, Chandler confessed he had used one of his *Action Detective* stories to teach himself how to write for the pulps:

> I simply made an extremely detailed synopsis of your story and from that rewrote it and then compared what I had with yours, and then went back and rewrote it some more, and so on. It looked pretty good. Incidentally, I found out the trickiest part of your technique was the ability to put over a situation which verged on the implausible but which in the reading seemed quite real. I hope you understand I mean this as a compliment. I have never come even near to doing it myself. Dumas had this quality in a very strong degree. Also Dickens.

To other correspondents Chandler liked to razz Gardner. About a scene in a Perry Mason novel having to do with the lawyer watching a young lady's legs he remarked, "The result has all the naughty charm—for me at any rate—of an elderly pervert surprised while masturbating in a public toilet." Chandler did admit, in another letter, that "I know him very well and like him." He couldn't refrain, however, from adding, "He is a terrible talker, just wears you out, but he is not a dull talker. He just talks too loud and too much. Years of yapping into a dictaphone machine have destroyed the quality of his voice, which now has all the delicate chiaroscuro of a French taxi horn."

Joseph Shaw left *Black Mask* in 1936, after refusing to take a salary cut. He was replaced by Fanny Ellsworth, who'd been editing the publisher's *Ranch Romances* pulp. In keeping with tradition, Miss Ellsworth appeared on the masthead as simply "F. Ellsworth," thus not betraying her gender. The price of the magazine was dropped from twenty to fifteen cents and the format was changed slightly. Under Shaw such artists as J. W. Schlaikjer, Fred Craft, and John Drew had supplied covers that were predominantly white, with straight-shooting figures often incomplete. With Ellsworth a band of color was used to frame watercolor paintings that were softer and more romantic. Arthur Rodman Bowker, who'd done all the interior illustrations during Shaw's term of office, continued to illustrate the stories in his stiff, scratchy, awkward style.

Chandler ceased contributing after Captain Shaw departed, but Gardner, Stinson, and many others stayed on. "Ellsworth certainly made an impressive start at her new job," comments William F. Nolan. "Within a space of just eight months, between January and September of 1937, she brought no less than nine impressive talents to the *Mask*. Among them: Cornell Woolrich, Max Brand, Frank Gruber, and Steve Fisher."

Ellsworth did seem to favor authors who weren't quite as rough as the gang of the early thirties. Fisher, for instance, felt that his stories were more subjective, less cold and detached. But "in the early days of the game that wasn't the popular trend, that kind of writing was like swimming upstream." Shaw had rejected Fisher, but Ellsworth bought nine of his stories during her four years in the editor's chair.

Gruber, a close friend of Fisher's, also did very well once Ellsworth arrived. Gruber sold her fourteen stories, ten of them about Oliver Quade the Human Encyclopedia. In his memoir of those days, *The Pulp Jungle*, Gruber recalled that Ellsworth had invited him to bring Quade to *Black Mask* and had agreed to his request for two cents a word. Quade, who was smart rather than tough, had made his debut in *Thrilling Detective* and would later serve as a model for Gruber's better known Johnny Fletcher. Understandably Gruber was fonder of Miss Ellsworth than of Cap Shaw. He said of her that she was "an extremely erudite woman. You would have thought she'd be more at home with a magazine like *Vogue* or *Harper's*." Both Gruber and Fisher went on to become very successful Hollywood screenwriters.

But the more subjective approach didn't help *Black Mask's* sales much. Early in 1940 Eltinge Warner sold the title to Henry Steeger's Popular Publications. "I bought *Black Mask* because I liked it," Steeger told me recently, adding that it proved to be a very successful title for him, as we'll see later on.

Chapter 4

"Brother, Can You Spare A Dime?"

The Depression and the hard-boiled private eye grew up together. From the time Wall Street laid an egg in 1929 until the United States entered World War II in 1941 over 160 detective pulps were introduced. A good number of them succeeded and almost every one had a bunch of P.I.'s in its lineup. The most important detective pulp, after *Black Mask*, was a child of the Depression. It sold, unlike most of the competition, for just ten cents.

The first issue of *Dime Detective* came out near the end of 1931, a bleak year in what was to be, in many ways, a grim decade. The Depression was continuing to grow worse and a stubborn and befuddled President Hoover seemed unable to cope with the nation's increasing economic problems. There were nearly 12 million unemployed in a country that then had a population of 122 million. Prohibition was still in effect; Al Capone was still out of jail. Jimmy Walker was mayor of New York; Adolf Hitler was moving ever closer to becoming chancellor of Germany. Bread lines and riots were getting to be familiar parts of urban life.

Henry Steeger and his partner, Harold Goldsmith, had been magazine publishers for a little over a year when *Dime Detective* was born. Still in his twenties, Steeger was a former employee of Dell Publishing. There he'd edited pulps and in 1929 became editor of George Delacorte's pioneering original-material comic book, the tabloid-size *The Funnies*. Goldsmith, who'd been with the Ace pulp outfit, and Steeger each put up $5,000 to found Popular Publications. Of their initial four titles introduced in 1930 two were in the detective category—*Detective Action Stories* and *Gang World*. The other two were *Western Rangers* and *Battle Aces*, the latter the magazine that eventually became the home of the noted aviator G-8.

Dime Detective was the cornerstone of a line of ten-cent pulpwoods—*Dime Western*, *Dime Mystery*, etc. By 1933 Popular was using the slogan "Twice as good—for half the price." A house ad explained the line this way:

> In these days when most of us are trying desperately to make half as much go twice as far, the instant success of Popular Publications' new group of dime magazines is not to be wondered at. There was never any doubt in our minds that there were just as many people who liked to read good red-blooded adventure fiction as there were in the old prosperity days. The problem was to give it to them at a depression price—without sacrificing the high quality which all readers of Popular Publications have learned to expect. We solved the problem. The magazine you now hold in your hands is one proof of that statement.

The initial issue of *Dime Detective*, cover-dated November 1931, included hard-boiled detective stories by Erle Stanley Gardner and Frederick Nebel, both frequent contributors to *Black Mask*, as well as material by T. T. Flynn and J. Alan Dunn. Dunn's "The Shadow of the Vulture" was firmly in the horror-mystery camp and there was to be at least one story of this type in every issue for quite a while. It's been suggested that, despite the spooky stuff, *Dime Detective* was meant to be an imitation of *Black Mask*. I talked recently to Henry Steeger about the beginnings of the magazine. "I wasn't aiming at any other book in particular," he told me. "I just wanted to get good detective stories, that's all." Steeger himself served as the first editor and his policy was "I picked out the best authors I could find—and I went after those I liked." He was willing to pay some of them fairly well. Nebel, for instance, was given four cents a word, which was a handsome rate then and more than *Black Mask* could offer him. Among the other early writers were John Lawrence, Oscar Schisgall, Fred MacIsaac, Edgar Wallace, and Carroll John Daly, who made his *Dime Detective* debut in the third issue.

From Daly's fertile imagination sprang Vee Brown, just about the only pulp character ever who was both a gun-wielding killer gumshoe and a successful writer of pop tunes. This new detective was a combination of Race Williams and Philo Vance, a sort of hard-boiled fop. Vee Brown was attached to the Manhattan D.A.'s office in some way, but carried on in the best dilettante private-eye fashion. The stories were narrated by a worshipful young man named Dean:

I had been associated with Vee Brown for some time and was still sharing his luxurious penthouse on top of one of Park Avenue's most pretentious apartment houses. Indeed, the lease was in my name, for no one but myself knew that the small, almost delicate detective, who was feared by all criminals, was also Vivian, the unknown writer of many of our most sentimental song hits, the enormous income of which he kept secret.

"Killer of Men" he was spoken of in the department and the criminal world. "Master of Melodies" he was called in Tin Pan Alley.

Vee's was not your ordinary pretentious penthouse and it seems probable he patronized the same interior decorator as Race:

Our penthouse was an impregnable fortress. Brown had always said that a man needed his sleep. When he retired at night great steel shutters covered the French windows that opened on the terrace. There were stone steps from that terrace leading to the locked gates below. The main entrance to the penthouse itself led to the hall—one floor above the elevators. That front door was lined with steel.

When not out on a case, Vee often lolled around his assault-proof apartment in a lounging robe and perused such items as a leather-bound volume of Dante. An unsolved mystery made him uneasy; an uncaught killer fouled up his other career. "While this murderer lives, it interferes with my work—my songs," he would explain. "You can't have murder and young love in your heart—at

least, not at the same time." Fiercely dedicated to the
detective side of his career, Vee often took on a job because
it afforded him an opportunity to act as a dispenser of
much-needed justice:

> Roberts muttered. And then, "I want to thank
> you for your interest in me."
> "In you?" Vee laughed. "Don't kid yourself
> about that. When this little affair is over you'll
> owe me nothing." He clenched his fingers tightly
> at his sides. "The Rock—perhaps the cleverest—
> certainly the slimiest of criminals. Others murder
> for him and he throws them to the wolves of the
> underworld that they may not betray him. Pro-
> tects himself behind the shadows of doped or half-
> maddened criminals, and when he kills, shoots
> men in the back. I've wanted for years to put a
> bullet in him. No, Mr. Roberts, I'll owe you a
> debt of gratitude."

In his own way he was as tough and violent as Race
Williams. For instance, in this scene wherein he deals with
some heavies who've conned Dean into letting them into
the penthouse:

> Three men—with guns drawn—passed between
> us and the machine gun toward the other side of
> the room.
> They never crossed that room. The tall man
> was facing Brown, his gun in his right hand,
> hanging by his side. There was a good fifteen feet
> between him and Brown. It was his face that told

the story more than his stifled cry. His gun went
up and his mouth opened. There was a terrific
roar close to my ear.

I think I blinked, but the tall man had a hole
where his left eye had been and he was falling,
even as the stocky man, swung, fired—and died
on his feet. Or in the air, rather, for he was
springing toward Vee Brown when his gun went
off. I didn't know what hit him then, but I knew
that it stopped him, held him there a moment.
Then another single shot roared and he twisted in
the air and crashed to the floor.

A tommy gun started and stopped—but I
wasn't watching Porky. I was watching Vee
Brown—standing there in those gay striped-silk
pajamas, a heavy revolver in each hand. Guns
that had killed two men and now . . .

As with most of Race Williams's shoot-outs, there was an
element of the miraculous in Vee Brown's gun battles with
the scum of the underworld. He, like Race, apparently
possessed the talents of a first-rank western gunslinger and
a top show business conjurer.

Daly wrote of two other detectives—Marty Day and
Clay Holt. Then in the summer of 1935 he transplanted
Race Williams from *Black Mask* to *Dime Detective*. "Was
the move prompted by a higher per-word rate?" speculates
Michael Barson. "Or had Cap Shaw at last grown weary of
stale plots and clunky prose?" Shaw was not fond of Daly's
work, but was reluctant to dump one of the magazine's still
very popular characters. When I asked Steeger about the
advent of Race Williams, he told me that he had invited

Daly to bring his character over. Steeger was well aware of the drawing power of the flamboyant op, which he was certain would continue at *Dime Detective*, and it did for several years. "Carroll and I got to know each other," Steeger added. "We really had a social club at the office, and it was one of the most informal offices in all of New York." According to him, a visitor to Popular Publications headquarters at 205 East Forty-second Street in the 1930s might encounter anything from a crap game to a Ping-Pong match, not to mention the dog which served as mascot.

Race Williams appeared twice in *Dime Detective* in 1935, four times in 1936, and fourteen more times between 1937 and 1940. He was often the subject of the cover painting and his name was always showcased in bold type on the front of every issue in which he was featured. The *Dime* Race was as tough and audacious as ever. And, as he was fond of reminding his readers, he did very well in his chosen profession:

> I was making plenty money these days—and most of it was easy money. I bought information for certain people and got paid to turn it over to them. Once in a while things got a bit tough, and a little shooting took place—but not too often, and not too tough.

And he made certain he collected on the spot:

> "It is my custom," I told him flat, "to take my fee immediately upon completion of the case."
> "Immediately?" His eyebrows went up. He looked strangely hurt and dignified and slightly surprised.

"Well," I gave him my pleasantest smile. "If you're busy right now, I won't insist." I sat down in a chair. "Suppose we say in fifteen minutes, then."

Race continued to work miracles with his .44s:

He just leveled the gun out with all the assurance in the world, tightened his finger on the trigger and said: "Race Williams—meet Ira Lent."

As for me, I closed the finger of my left hand—a split second and the finger of my right hand closed. A forty-four is a heavy gun. Bert didn't fire again. Before I hit the floor he had picked himself up in the air, clawed at his chest with both hands, and gone hurtling across the room.

"You *were* Ira Lent," I said.

"Come on," he snarled as if he were talking to a common pickpocket, "tell me where that girl's hiding before I blow you apart." Then he raised his eyes and looked straight into my face. "God— Race Williams," he said, and his fingers tightened on the triggers of twin guns.

So I shot him twice right in the chest.

He fired all right. I couldn't shoot that fast. But my bullets had picked him right up and tossed him into the air when his guns went off. Perhaps he put out a star or two—but not me.

Another tough private eye who blazed his way across the pages of the magazine was Jack Cardigan, the creation of

Frederick Nebel. "The big op from the Cosmos Detective Agency" showed up in *Dime Detective* more than any other series character. Cardigan was there in the first issue, and forty-four stories and novelets about him were featured from 1931 to 1937. Originally he'd played a second lead character, a cop, in a Captain MacBride story in *Black Mask*. Graduating to a star position, Cardigan got rougher and much less patient. He was rude, restless, streetwise, and shrewd. It was his steadfast policy not to take any crap from anybody, no matter which side of the law that person was on. He was a genuine tough guy and sure of it. Therefore he didn't, like Race Williams, feel compelled to brag about the fact.

Nebel wrote about Cardigan in the quirky, wisecracking third-person style that was his version of the hard-boiled manner. The Cardigan cases, which add up to well over a half million words of first-rate prose, were never gathered into a book, and not one of them has ever been reprinted. Today, though a much abler operative than the majority of his contemporaries, Cardigan is just about forgotten.

A partner in the Cosmos Agency, Cardigan was a restless, footloose man. In the course of his six-year career he managed agency branch offices in various cities across the country and also worked on a number of out-of-town jobs. His favorite spots were San Francisco and New York City, but he also operated in St. Louis and an assortment of composite cities in the Midwest and New England. His first case was "Death Alley" (November 1931), which found him running the Cosmos office in St. Louis; his last was "No Time to Kill" (May 1937), which took place in Wheelburg, a fictitious industrial city he'd worked in before. The senior partner was George Hammerhorn, based in Manhattan,

who tried, without much long-term success, to be a
calming and stabilizing influence on the big, hotheaded
Cardigan.

Often Cardigan teamed up with an attractive lady
operative named Pat Seaward. Their relationship was
similiar to that which is popular on several current
television crime shows: they were obviously fond of each
other but nothing much ever came of it. Cardigan was far
from dapper and Nebel sometimes used Pat to emphasize
the point:

> The train from New York dragged slowly through
> the St. Louis yards in the smoky winter dusk.
> Snow had fallen all the way from Indianapolis.
> The coaches, the Pullmans were white-blanketed;
> the hissing locomotive was flecked and spattered
> with the snow and the bell had a lazy, bonging
> sound.
>
> Cardigan was standing in the vestibule of the
> head sleeper, cuddling a cigarette in his palm. His
> battered fedora was cramped low on his forehead,
> his old ulster was wrinkled, its shapeless collar
> bundled about his neck.
>
> Pat Seaward, small, trim in a three-quarter
> length raccoon, with a racy antelope beret aslant
> on her head, came out of the corridor. She said:
> "You certainly look as though you slept in those
> clothes."
> "I did, precious, more than once."

Besides being several notches below a fashion plate,
Cardigan didn't lead an especially exemplary personal life,

the effects of which his colleagues often had to suffer through:

Cardigan loomed in the doorway of the Cosmos Agency at eleven A.M.., banged through the wooden gate, sailed past the secretary, the office boy, two file clerks, and wound up in the private office of George Hammerhorn, who was studying a set of fingerprints.

Patricia Seaward sat in one of the leather chairs, a patent-leather traveling bag beside her. Cardigan grunted "Hello" to both, went on to an alcove back of a screen, mixed baking-soda with water, downed the concoction. As he rinsed the glass, he burped, muttered, "Excuse me," but to no one in particular. Then he said, "Ah," but this to himself, the ravages of indigestion having been put to sleep.

He wore a baggy blue serge suit, no vest; a soft white shirt with collar attached and a badly arranged black bowtie. His bashed and battered fedora had once been steel-gray but now it resembled something that might have been kicked around the street and then left hanging in a tree during the rainy season. He took it as he reappeared from behind the screen and sailed it into a chair.

George Hammerhorn, stocky, well-pressed, said without looking up: "Does it take you two hours to get from Thirty-seventh Street to Fifty-third?"

"Did it take me two hours?"

"Exactly."

"Then it must take two hours, George."

Despite his tardiness in showing up at the office, Cardigan usually moved fast when he was actually on a case. He could often be seen pushing his way into places:

> He slapped open the heavy glass swing-door and a gust of winter wind came in with him. He headed up the high, narrow lobby, rain dripping from his battered brown fedora, his old ulster pungent with the smell of damp wool.

Quite frequently Cardigan wasn't especially welcome. But that didn't faze him, not for long, as we see in this heave-ho from a speakeasy:

> As he reached the bottom step a hand gripped him on either side and he looked up to find himself flanked by two gorillas.
>
> "It's out, brother," one of them said.
>
> "You can walk," the other said, "out the front door. Or we use the back door for throw-outs. I'd say use the front. The back's a long drop. . . ."
>
> One opened the door and Cardigan stood there drawing on his gloves. He took his time. One of the gorillas became impatient and used a foot. Cardigan stumbled down four steps, grabbed the handrail and braced himself. The door banged.

He stood for a moment rubbing himself. Then he climbed the steps again and rang the bell. The door opened and the gorilla who had kicked him stuck his head out.

Cardigan hit him square in the mouth and drove him half the length of the entrance hall. Then he reached in, grabbed the knob and closed the door. He walked a block and felt better.

It's likely that Cardigan made some of the most memorable involuntary exits in the pulps, as, for example, in this departure from a Russian Hill apartment in Frisco:

The gang charged and Cardigan went down under five who were youths in everything but heft and punch. Drawing his gun was out of the question; so was trying to reason with five drunks. By sheer numbers—and two of the lads were as big and husky as he was—Cardigan was carried to the door amid a downpour of blows.

"O.K., Charlie! Remember how we used to put the shot, old kid, old pal, old sock. Ready! *Eins, zwei, drei!* . . ."

Cardigan felt himself sailing through free air. He cleared the porch railing, twisting; caromed off the staircase balustrade, slammed into the steps. He tried to stop himself, but went head over heels down the steps, shot into space again and landed on a balustrade below, cracking, breaking it; fell plummetlike again and crashed into hard earth and loose stones, rolled and slid downward and came to an abrupt stop against a

pillar of a lower switchback in the staircase.
Bruised, dazed, half senseless, he lay there
panting hoarsely, long tears in his overcoat, his
hat gone.

"Boy-oh-boy!" he muttered, and again, "Boy-oh-boy!"

Cardigan was a complete professional and, if he had to,
he could devote hours to a stakeout or to the patient
checking out of suspects. His sense of justice was his own
and not something that was handed down from above. The
Cosmos Agency handled everything from kidnaping to
arson to insurance fraud, and Cardigan was good at
cracking every sort of case. He made it clear to clients that
usually he was motivated by money: "I'm not in this
business because I like it." He was capable of cooperating
with the cops, but he was fond of very few of them, and if
he felt he'd been double-crossed, then all bets were off:
"Forget it, Brokhard. You were tough and nasty earlier
tonight. You were wise—a smart guy. O.K.—now you try
doing handsprings for awhile. I wouldn't tell you anything,
Brokhard. I wouldn't even tell you the time."

The Cosmos dick was Nebel's final pulp character. He
moved on to the better-paying slicks, becoming a frequent
contributor to *Collier's*, *This Week*, *Redbook*, *Cosmopolitan*, and other magazines. But he never wrote anything this
good again.

Kenneth Sheldon White took over as editor of *Dime
Detective* in the mid-thirties. Probably the only second-generation pulp editor in the business, he was the son of
Trumbull White, who had served as the first editor of
Adventure back in 1910. Some of White's contributors

shared W. T. Ballard's opinion that "he tried to copy *Black Mask* with *Dime Detective.*" Certainly White tried to lure Gardner, Daly, Roger Torrey, George Harmon Coxe, John K. Butler, and other regulars away from his chief rival. But he also brought in people like William E. Barrett, Robert Sidney Bowen, Dale Clark, Hugh B. Cave, and D. L. Champion. He allowed the gifted Norbert Davis to write the sort of comedy detective stories that he was best at, something neither Shaw nor Fanny Ellsworth did over at *Black Mask.*

White, although devoted to series characters, never turned the magazine completely over to private eyes or even to hard-boiled fiction. There was always room for what was then known as the off-trail story. One of the most individual of writers in the detective pulp field was Cornell Woolrich. Ken White was among the earliest of pulpwood editors to buy his stuff. Woolrich's stories dealt ostensibly with the props and premises of crime fiction—with murder, robbery, revenge—yet they were really anxious parables about loneliness, death, and the unexpected darkness that can suddenly close in on life.

I met Woolrich toward the end of his life and spent a few rather forlorn evenings watching him drink himself into a stupor in various Manhattan bars, usually saloons with the initials P. J. in the name. By that time he professed to be indifferent to his writing, and on several occasions he expressed scorn for a scholarly type who kept trying to get him to talk about his novels and stories. For some reason, though, he didn't mind talking to me about his life and work, filling me in on just about everything he'd ever written. What had made his wild, improbable books and stories so successful, I think, was that they were actually fantasies, imagined with that feverish intensity Woolrich conjured up when writing. I remember being surprised when I asked him about a story of his called "You Take Ballistics," and he mentioned that he'd never been in a police station in his life—"I just thought about what it would be like." Similarly he claimed he'd never ridden a subway, never smoked marijuana, never encountered a practitioner of voodoo. "My first novel took place in a nightclub," he added. "When I wrote it, I'd never been in one."

Back then I thought that Woolrich, as he grew increasingly tipsy, was weaving a few fantasies for me. But I found out long after his death that many of the seemingly incredible yarns he told me were true. "I was married for a few weeks once in Hollywood," he mentioned one night, "but I didn't like it." Turns out, according to a biographical account by Francis M. Nevins, that he really had been: "While in Hollywood [in 1930], Woolrich fell in love with and married a producer's daughter, who left him after a few weeks and later had the marriage annulled."

Undoubtedly the saddest of the sad young men of the F. Scott Fitzgerald generation, Woolrich broke into print in the twenties with a series of novels and short stories about flappers and philosophers. He was dominated by his mother and lived with her thoughout her life, chiefly in Manhattan hotel suites. By the early 1930s he felt he had to try new markets for his work. The Jazz Age was long gone; the Depression had enfeebled or destroyed many of his markets; even Fitzgerald wasn't doing that well anymore. According to Nevins, Woolrich was never in need of money, thanks to his mother's financial position. When he talked to me about this period of his life, though, I got the impression that he felt he had to keep selling and seeing his work in print. Looking around for new outlets, he was persuaded to try the detective pulps. He wrote some short stories and took them around himself to the editorial offices. And he began to sell again. *Detective Fiction Weekly* published his first two stories in the mystery field. *Dime Detective* used his third, as well as his fourth, fifth, and sixth. The magazine and White turned out to be very hospitable to Woolrich, eventually buying more of his work than any other pulp except *DFW*. Over thirty of his dark tales were used there from 1934 to 1944.

Another writer welcomed by Kenneth White was Raymond Chandler. Chandler had remained loyal to Joseph Shaw for as long as the captain was in charge of *Black Mask*, even though he apparently harbored some doubts about his editorial acumen. In a 1946 letter to Erle Stanley Gardner, Chandler said:

> I also agree with you that he was blind to any kind of writing he did not think the best at the moment. I don't believe Cornell Woolrich or Cleve Adams ever made *BM* under his editorship, although both were probably far better men than some of his regulars. Norbert Davis also, who took his murders rather lightly when allowed, made the *BM* only two or three times. He said Shaw was too fussy for him and took the whole thing too seriously. I'm quite sure Shaw would never have published a story I once wrote kidding the pants off the tough dick story, but Ken White did.

While *Dime Detective* was open to the lighter sort of detective story, what Chandler actually wrote for the magazine—with the exception of that kidding story "Pearls Are a Nuisance"—was more of his usual hard-boiled, poetic private-eye yarns. He sold seven stories to White from 1937 to 1939, five of them first-person narratives about a private eye named John Dalmas. Dalmas was Philip Marlowe in everything but name. He was tough, sardonic, and given to seeing Southern California as no one else did. The Dalmas stories were "Mandarin's Jade," "Bay City Blues," "Trouble Is My Business," "The Lady in the Lake," and "Red Wind," this last containing one of Chandler's most memorable openings:

> There was a desert wind blowing that night. It was one of those hot dry Santa Anas that come down through the mountain passes and curl your hair and make your nerves jump and your skin itch. On nights like that every booze party ends in a fight. Meek little wives feel the edge of the carving knife and study their husbands' necks. Anything can happen. You can even get a full glass of beer at a cocktail lounge.

Roger Torrey, like some of his colleagues—notably Woolrich and Chandler—was a heavy drinker. His escapades on both coasts earned him a certain notoriety in the thirties and forties. In a recent interview, for example, Carroll John Daly's daughter-in-law recalled the time that "he and Roger Torrey—a pretty good friend of his—were trying to borrow fifteen dollars from Dashiell Hammett. They were drunk and he wouldn't give it to them. So they broke his plate-glass window." Although his personal reputation suffered because of his escapades, Torrey was always able to turn out good stories. He hit *Black Mask* fifty times, during the reigns of three different editors. To *Dime Detective* he sold eleven from 1934 to 1941.

An old drinking buddy of his once assured me that his last name was originally "Torres" and that he'd changed it when he embarked on his writing career in 1932. Torrey, however, always maintained he was "Irish by descent." He'd lived the sort of early life that always looks great summed up in a dust jacket biography:

> Three years of high school. Canadian army at sixteen. A year in a bank. Then working in a sawmill, then keeping time and books in a logging camp. Then playing piano in a theatre. Graduated, or maybe it was going the other way, into a theatre organist and worked at this until talking pictures killed this business. This took me up and down the West Coast and as far east as Tulsa, Oklahoma, though most of the time was spent in San Francisco and Los Angeles. Ran a show on the Klamath Indian Reservation until 1930. Then many things . . . starving and pick and shovel and driving a truck among them.

He once informed readers of *Dime Detective* that "writing crime fiction came natural. When the music business was good, every musician got around to a lot of places and met a lot of the (lower?) element, and I used to be insane about gambling, which same habit took me to even other places that serve as a base for local color. Also have chummed around with several policemen."

Several of his stories for the magazine were about a private eye named Johnny Carr (aka Johnny Cass in the earlier ones). These were in the present tense, in a variation of the approach used by such writers as J. J. des Ormeaux and Damon Runyon:

> I can't see it's any time to fool around and try any trick shoulder shots or hooey like that. His face is about the size of a dinner plate and about twenty-five feet away and I bore him as near the center of it as I can hit. He comes down on what's left of it like somebody drops a sack of wheat. All in a bunch. I drop the opal he gives me right after the brawl starts and don't figure I've got time to look for it so I grab the case that's got the other one in it and stop by him and turn him over to get my gun. He's fallen on it and I can't leave it because the number is registered on my concealed-weapon permit.
>
> And then I get a shock.
>
> I turn him over and find I've caught him right in the puss. I shoot a .45 and it's made a hell of a mess and on the floor underneath his mouth in a lot of blood are those pretty teeth he showed so damn much of when he smiled. Uppers and lowers. Both false and both smashed. I pick up the gun and the teeth and take a powder.

Norbert Davis sold only five stories to the magazine in the thirties. It wasn't until the early forties that he began to appear more frequently. The early work in *Dime Detective* was relatively serious. His first story was entitled "The Gin Monkey" (January 15, 1935) and was about a tough private detective hunting for the killer of a drunken sculptor. Davis could do this sort of stuff very well, in a casual, cinematic style that allowed for a lazy but effective approach to violence:

> Max Clark looked thin and dark and dapper, showing his white teeth in a smile, leaning forward. There were glittering, excited lights deep back in his brown eyes. The .38 police revolver in his hand caught the slanting rays of sunlight from the window and glinted prettily as he moved it. He pointed the revolver at Borzig's stomach and watched him and smiled his wise, knowing smile, quirking up one corner of his mouth and shutting one eye.
>
> Borzig coughed once, apologetically, and backed up until his knees hit the edge of the couch and sat down suddenly. He looked up, and his eyes were very large. He made unbelieving noises to himself and tugged at his wilted collar in an aimless way.

All sorts of other private investigators practiced in *Dime Detective* during its first decade. There were John Lawrence's Sam Beckett, Jan Dana's Acme Indemnity Op, Hugh B. Cave's Peter Kane. D. L. Champion began his Inspector Allhoff series in 1938, introducing a nasty, coffee-swilling, legless ex-cop who was still associated, though not quite officially, with the New York police. Allhoff was literally an armchair detective. As Bill Pronzini mentions in *The Arbor House Treasury of Detective & Mystery Stories from the Great Pulps*, Champion "took the Nero Wolfe formula and gave it a perverse twist." Among Erle Stanley Gardner's several sleuths were Dane Skarle and Go Get 'Em Garver.

Dime Detective did very well from the start, always among Steeger's top-selling magazine titles. Early in 1933 it was decided to increase the schedule to twice a month. An announcement explained:

> The flood of letters from you readers was what did the trick, what made us realize that twelve copies a year were not anywhere near enough to satisfy the demand we had created for our particular brand of ace-high detective fiction. . . . Twenty-four issues a year—ten cents a copy—and a hundred percent quality! That's what you have to look forward to and if you ask us it's a pretty bright outlook for any detective-fiction fan. . . . One thin dime planked down on your news dealer's counter on the First and Fifteenth of every month is a sure way to get the utmost in thrill fiction.

During its first years *Dime Detective* was packaged like a horror rather than a detective pulp. The standard cover scene, as Robert Kenneth Jones points out in *The Shudder Pulps*, showed "the heroine in some state of undress, and being subjected to various indignities." On the April 15, 1935, cover a spread-eagled young lady in a low-cut gown is about to have molten metal poured over her by a pair of highly sinister Orientals; on the November 1935 cover a strapped-down young lady wearing little more than a few bandages is about to be operated on by a surgeon dressed entirely in black; on the February 1933 cover a naked young lady has already been frozen solid in a block of ice. And so it went. Later in the thirties, especially after Popular introduced *Dime Mystery*, a magazine devoted entirely to horror, the damsel-in-distress motif was not used for every single issue. Cardigan was the subject of some covers, as was Race Williams, and there were even a few covers without a woman in them at all.

William Reusswig, Malvin Singer, and Walter Baumhofer painted the majority of the covers. Their paintings are bright and bold, making rich use of the most popular cover colors—red and yellow. An effective pulp cover always had the same come-on effect as a circus poster or an ad for the next chapter of a movie serial. All the interior illustrations, one per story, thoughout the thirties were by John Fleming Gould. His work was passable at best and the only evidence of any versatility came when he botched drawings in a variety of rendering techniques. He also had the notion that all tough detectives were ugly and wore rumpled clothes.

In the summer of 1935, after more than two years as a biweekly, *Dime Detective* dropped back to a once-per-month schedule and remained a monthly throughout the 1940s.

Chapter 5

The Hard-boiled Decade

Providing cheap thrills is almost always a road to success. The pulp industry, like most businesses that offered low-cost entertainment, was stimulated by the Depression. During the first five years of the thirties alone, for instance, over eighty new mystery and crime pulps were introduced, ranging from *Popular Detective* and *Headquarters Detective* to *Speakeasy Stories* and *Scotland Yard. Nickel Detective* gave it a try in 1931, and Nick Carter returned in a pulp of his own in 1933. During the early years of the decade several of the notable mystery men also made their debuts, gents such as the Shadow, the Spider, and Secret Agent X. But most of all, the thirties were the decade of the hard-boiled detective.

Of all the new detective pulps launched in the early 1930s, none tried harder to look like a twin of *Black Mask* than Fiction House's *Black Aces*. The outfit even hired artist Fred Craft to whip up the same sort of unfinished, white-background covers he painted for their successful rival. Cap Shaw ran an editorial page at the front of each issue of *Black Mask*, signed boldly "The Editor," and *Black Aces* had one, too. In the first number the editor explained, in prose that was a mite flowery for the headman of a tough detective pulp, why this new pulp was "the Story Magazine of the World's Lone Wolves":

> Since the first mists of time the man who ran out of the pack has been a front page story. Always a threat to the established order of things he has been a marked figure in every age. The drum of the chase has ever sounded in his ears. . . . He is the Lone Wolf—the man who for one reason or other fights the common fight for us all. Beyond the temptation of money or place he meets the criminal on even terms. He is the Black Ace— society's flaming sword. Here in these pages the leading writers of the day will tell you the stories of the Black Aces.

The magazine cost twenty cents a copy, the same as *Black Mask*. In its issues were stories by Erle Stanley Gardner, Eugene Cunningham, and Theodore Tinsley, all of whom were *Black Mask* regulars. George Bruce was also present. Prolific and versatile, he even had a pulp named after him—*George Bruce's Air Novels*, another Fiction House venture. His detective was a tough Broadway cop named Nick Rongetti: "He was tall and thin and swarthy. . . . His voice was unpleasant. . . . His hair was startling in its whiteness above the man's dark face. A purple birthmark covered the left side of his forehead almost to the ear." While on stakeouts Rongetti was sometimes to be seen reading a copy of the *Christian Science Guardian*.

Theodore Tinsley came up with a variation, a fairly rough and bloody one, of Edgar Wallace's "Four Just Men" for *Black Aces*. Major John Tattersall Lacy had commanded the 697th Machine Gun Battalion during the Great War. Readers were told:

> His eyes were alert and stamped with authority. He was clean-shaven except for a trim, sandy mustache that imperfectly concealed a scar that curved like a small white crescent from his upper lip past his nostril. The scar was no disfigurement; on the contrary, it gave a curiously arresting and vital quality to his smile. Women found that smile of his disturbing and rather thrilling, but Jack Lacy was completely unaware of women. From head to foot, in thought and habit, he was a man's man.

Returning to New York after adventuring around the world, the major is hired by a group of rich and influential citizens calling themselves the Emergency Council. They want him to head up a vigilante committee to wipe out organized crime in Manhattan: "Hitherto we've worked with the law. From now on our program will be different. . . . What we seek now is the knowledge, detection and extermination of the racketeer."

Major Lacy agrees and recruits a handful of his former army buddies to form an attack force. They are housed atop the tallest structure in the city, called the Cloud Building in the stories, and it seems likely that Lester Dent remembered the major and his crew when he had the gang from his first Doc Savage pulp novel headquartered in the

Empire State Building. Unlike Doc, Major Lacy and company concentrated on combating gangsters and left supervillains alone.

The major was extremely rough on crooks, showing them no mercy, as, for example, when he caught up with an arsonist who was beating a retreat down a fire escape:

> Harry Lipper reached the lowest fire escape and threw one leg anchor-like over the railing. Twenty feet below him was a stone-paved court, flanked by whitewashed walls on either side; and in the rear, a wooden fence. The racket boss jerked out a thirty-eight police positive and raised his arm upward like a flash. But he was miles too late.
>
> The major's bullet burned through coat and vest and pierced his heart.
>
> His fat leg unhooked slowly from the railing. He fell head first to the concrete below, and lay there in a curiously huddled heap, like a man trying to stand on his head.

The boss of New York's rackets turned out to be a gangster with the splendid name of Francis Assisi. By the time of the final novelet in the series, Assisi and his minions had caused considerable damage to the major's crew:

> My associate and friend, Ed Corning, is slowly recovering his strength in a private hospital on West End Avenue. Assisi shot him in the back. Captain Harrigan, of my staff, was kidnapped and

tortured—his hands and feet burned with flame. That was two weeks ago and poor Harrigan is now barely able to take a few tottering steps.

On top of this, Dillon, Major Lacy's closest friend and associate, is gunned down in the street by a tommy gunner riding in the back of a hijacked ambulance. Commandeering a taxicab, Lacy gives chase:

> He saw the skidding ambulance slow, swerve far out to the west curb, and make a long skidding turn toward the side street.
>
> His hands closed hard on the wheel.
>
> He never hesitated an instant. He was frenzied, apish. With a hoarse growl in his throat he sent his cab screaming straight for the turning ambulance.
>
> The accelerator was down to the floor. He took a single deep breath and waited, with body braced.
>
> His steel-shod juggernaut struck the side of the ambulance.

Finally, after getting over that collision, the major catches up with Assisi himself:

> Lacy was on him like a stag-hound. Teeth sank into his wrist, but he smashed at the bloody mouth with his free hand and caught the squirming throat again. His knee lifted and anchored the criminal against the table. . . . Suddenly Assisi screamed. A shrill woman-sound. It was followed

by a sharp crack like a dry stick. Lacy's hands came slowly away. The body slid grotesquely to the floor.

"That," said Lacy in a dull, sing-song groan, "is the way that soldiers kill vermin . . ."

In an interview nearly half a century later, Tinsley recalled that his brother, illustrator Frank Tinsley, had lent a hand with the Lacy saga:

My brother's sole contribution was to sit down with me . . . with a lot of glorious back-and-forth talk between us as we battled out a bunch of wild probabilities with a thin veneer of "sure it could have happened, if you knew good old Major Lacy." Frank had a good sense of invention (and sure he didn't have to write it), a bunch of wild ideas that I had to clothe in some sort of believability. He knew a lot of salty National Guard characters.

Black Aces ceased after its seventh issue (July 1932), and early in 1933 Fiction House suspended all its publications, explaining that "the influx of lower-priced magazines and the incidental cheapening of the product has created a market situation that is unsound." A reorganized Fiction House returned later in the 1930s.

Not all detective pulps were interested in being tough during this predominantly hard-boiled decade. A few strove to offer more genteel fare. One such was *Great Detective*, a one-man operation published by William Levine under his own name and edited by him under his mystery-writing pen name of Will Levinrew. This fifteen-cent monthly, introduced early in 1933, offered quieter material, most of it reprinted—though usually neither the editor nor the publisher got around to mentioning that fact. "The 1920s still dominated its pages," points out Robert Sampson in *Mystery, Detective and Espionage Magazines*, "and the English mystery was the arbiter of quality." Dorothy L. Sayers's Lord Peter Wimsey appeared at least twice, Agatha Christie's Miss Marple three times. There were stories by G. K. Chesterton, Sax Rohmer, and E. W. Hornung. Ellery Queen wrote about Ellery Queen. Even Edgar Allan Poe was represented. The magazine folded after its ninth issue.

Just as Levinrew's magazine was expiring, a similar one came along. It even did business out of the same Chicago address. *The Mystery League Magazine*, which took its name from the Mystery League book publishing operation, was even more ambitious than *Great Detective*, featuring brand-new material and edited by Frederic Dannay and Manfred B. Lee under their Ellery Queen alias. Among the authors included in its pages were Dashiell Hammett, Phoebe Atwood Taylor, Gavin Holt, Charles G. Booth, and both Barnaby Ross and Ellery Queen. The cost per copy was twenty-five cents, a hefty price then for a pulp that provided neither weird horror yarns nor pictures of girls in their underwear. The magazine succumbed with its fourth issue. Commenting many years later, Lee said, "We were its entire staff . . . we did not even have a secretary. We selected the stories, prepared copy, read proofs, dummied, sweated, etc., and almost literally swept out the office as well. The magazine . . . died of insufficient where-withal."

The Illustrated Detective Magazine began late in 1929, changed its name to *The Mystery Magazine* in 1932, and lasted until the summer of 1935. Not a pulp at all, it was printed on slick paper and illustrated with both drawings and posed photographs. What it resembled most closely in format was a true-confessions magazine. It cost a dime and published stories by many of the pulp writers, including Frederick Nebel, H. Bedford Jones, Walter Ripperger, and Hulbert Footner. Ellery Queen wrote for the magazine, as did Mignon Eberhart, Vincent Starrett, Stuart Palmer, and Albert Payson Terhune. There were reprints of Dickens, Dumas, and Gaboriau.

Illustrated Detective/Mystery was one of four magazines introduced during the Christmas season of 1929 by Tower Magazines. The others were *New Movie*, *The Home*, and *Illustrated Love*. The boss of Tower was Catherine McNellis, once described by *Business Week* as "the dark little merchandising wizard from Wilkes-Barre." What the little wizard had done, at the same time as the Depression got going, was to convince the Woolworth chain to sell her magazines in their stores. The five-and-ten-cent stores became the major outlet for the ten-cent periodicals, and from the start the quartet had a combined monthly sale of over a million copies. Initially *Illustrated Detective* was slanted toward women, "but at its peak in the early 1930s," points out Sampson, "it offered material carefully calculated to appeal to most tastes and both sexes."

Aaron A. Wyn was another publisher who believed that what the country needed was a good ten-cent pulp. In the pulpwood business since the mid-1920s, he founded Magazine Publishers, Inc., in 1928, and in 1930 he bought the failing *Dragnet* from Harold Hersey. The title was first changed to *Detective-Dragnet* and then to *Ten Detective Aces*. At that point the price was dropped from fifteen to ten cents and Wyn adopted the slogans "10 Stories 10¢" and "A Cent a Story!" Up until the spring of 1933 the company used a swastika as an identifying symbol on covers and contents pages, but the rising notoriety of another group using the crooked cross caused Wyn to abandon it. All the subsequent mystery titles—such as *Gold Seal Detective*, *10-Story Detective*, and *Secret Agent X*—were priced at a dime.

What *Ten Detective Aces* presented was an amalgam of hard-boiled detective stories and somewhat weirder tales featuring mystery men and masked avengers. A star performer among the writers was Lester Dent, whose detectives were both tough and strange. For *Detective-Dragnet* there had been Lynn Lash, a scientific detective who dealt with the sort of problems that Operator #5 and the Spider would eventually confront. In "The Sinister Ray," for instance, Lash was up against what the blurb described as "Slant-eyed Orientals, malice missionaries of a Far East power, who plunged New York into a glittering light of darkness. Riding a crest of an ominous tidal wave, they swept the city—threatened to engulf the world." Dent's scientific detective in *Ten Detective Aces* was Lee Nace: "Lee Nace was a tall man, so gaunt he had a hungry look. His face was angular, solemn, almost puritanical. His attire was dark, very plain. He might have been mistaken for a minister." Nace had to cope with mutilated corpses of men boiled in oil, skeleton hands that tried to pull him into a coffin, and a villain known as the Green Skull.

Both Paul Chadwick and Norvell Page produced series about detectives whose caseloads were stranger than those of your average hard-boiled op. Chadwick's Wade Hammond was "a sort of Sam Spade/Richard Wentworth (aka the Spider) conglomerate," as Garyn G. Roberts suggests in his anthology *A Cent a Story!* "Hammond was one of the most popular, enduring characters ever to come from a Wyn magazine." Chadwick graduated to a pulp of his own—*Secret Agent X*. Page's detective was Ken Carter, a long, lean fellow who'd once been a professional juggler.

An even stranger crime fighter was Frederick C. Davis's Steve Thatcher. A police detective sergeant by profession, he was also the mysterious avenger known as the Moon Man. Not only was he a policeman, but his father was one as well. In fact, old Peter Thatcher was chief of police, though unaware of his son's alter ego. Chief Thatcher and the rest of the force thought of Moon Man as nothing better than a "notorious criminal who robbed the rich" and overlooked the Robin Hood aspects of his escapades. Young Steve Thatcher had one of the more striking mystery men getups:

> Watching the door, Thatcher quickly opened the small case he had carried in. From it he unrolled a long, voluminous black robe. He drew it over his shoulders swiftly. On his hands he pulled black gloves. He lifted carefully from the suitcase a sphere of silver glass—the precious mask of the Moon Man—and placed it over his head. Steve Thatcher vanished and the Moon Man appeared.

Recalling the days of such adventures as "Badge of Blood," "The Bleeding Skeleton," and "Ghoul's Gamble," Davis once told me:

I don't remember exactly where the Moon Man idea came from except that at the time Argus [one-way] glass was a novelty, and I was always looking for novelties. Once at a luncheon of writers A. A. Wyn gave an informal talk in which he pointed out that some writers follow a theme. He mentioned one whose heroes always worked at great risk outside the law in order to further justice. He meant me. That was exactly the pattern of the Moon Man.

The stories ran in every issue from June 1933 through March 1936. The last few appeared every other month, the final one in January 1937.

The more bizarre investigators faded from *Ten Detective Aces* in the late thirties. Such *Black Mask* regulars as W. T. Ballard, Dwight V. Babcock, and Frank Gruber provided more traditional hard-boiled fare. Another sometime contributor was a young writer who signed himself R. B. S. Davis. As Bob Davis he went on to draw and write for the burgeoning comic book industry. His work appeared in early Marvel titles and he did the Chameleon for *Target Comics* and Dick Cole for *Blue Bolt*.

Wyn added another ten-for-ten magazine early in 1938 with *10-Story Detective*, a bimonthly similar in looks and content to the *Ten Detective Aces* of the period. An even bigger bargain came along in the summer of the year, when *Variety Detective* was introduced and offered "12 Stories 10¢." In these years Magazine Publishers was doing quite well, with a combined circulation on all its titles of about a million copies each month. Wyn was described in the pages of *The Literary Digest* as being so busy that he had "scant time for supervising the gardening at his estate on Long Island or adding to his collection of antique ivories."

The enterprising Martin Goodman had entered pulp publishing early in the decade. He often unsettled his colleagues by openly stating such opinions as "fans are not interested in quality." In 1937, aiming to outdo *Ten Detective Aces*, Goodman brought out *Detective Short Stories* as part of his Red Star line and emblazoned the slogan "12 Stories for Ten Cents" on the cover. Although the ten-center claimed to be a bimonthly, it only managed to appear twenty-five times in the six years it existed.

The pulp was initially another of those mixes of hardboiled detective stories and the wilder weird-menace sort of stuff. Goodman also had *Mystery Tales*, devoted entirely to this latter type of material. Many of the covers of the detective magazine, built around scantily clad young women, slavering monsters, and battered heroes, could have graced the horror magazine. When asked by *Writer's Digest* what sort of material he was looking for, editor Robert Erisman replied, "Get sex into the story from the first paragraph." His regular writers, however—men like William R. Cox, Hugh B. Cave, W. T. Ballard, Dale Clark, and Roger Torrey—didn't always go along with that. They turned out their regular stories of two-fisted cops and P.I.'s, sometimes adding a bit more sex and violence than usual. Torrey was especially good at getting into a gruesome mood, as he did in a tale entitled "Blood of the Beast" (April 1938). The private eye finds a corpse while hiking up a rainswept roadway to call on his client:

> For a second I felt sick. Very sick. The girl was facing toward me and her throat was torn and hanging open and blood was still spouting from

the big artery there. Even in the few seconds the
match flickered I could see this flow grow weaker
and almost stop.

I just knelt there and shivered and it wasn't
from the wind and rain. If it had been broad
daylight I don't believe it would have hit me as
hard, but at that, I don't know. I've seen people
shot. I've seen people cut with knives and razors.
I've seen people taken out of wrecked cars;
people who looked like raw meat. But this girl's
throat had been TORN. Just ripped as though by
a giant hand.

As happened with other similarly inclined magazines, the
weird material was eventually dropped. Goodman, who
started the company that became Marvel Comics, used
some of his comic book artists as illustrators. Both Joe
Simon and Jack Kirby, creators of Captain America,
illuminated the pages of *Detective Short Stories*.

Blue Ribbon Magazines, Inc., which exists today as
Archie Comics, Inc., published several detective titles in
the 1930s, including *Undercover Detective*, *Double-Action
Detective*, and *Detective Yarns*. This last was a ten-cent
bimonthly launched in the spring of 1938. It, too, aimed at
keeping up with the competition and promised "12 Stories
10¢." W. T. Ballard, William Bogart, Roger Torrey, and
Wyatt Blassingame were some of the authors. A nonfiction
piece was often included among the hard-boiled yarns,
some contributed by a fellow with the admirable pen name
of "Undercover" Dix.

Publisher Ned Pines and his editorial director, Leo
Margulies, were essentially the juvenile's friends, and most

of their pulps were aimed at younger readers. Such titles as *The Phantom Detective*, started in 1933, and *Black Book Detective*, which showcased the Black Bat from 1939 on, were aimed directly at youthful minds. In 1931, at the request of a distributor, Pines went into pulp publishing with a line of dime magazines. The first two were *Thrilling Love Stories* and *Thrilling Detective*. This latter title was somewhat less adolescent. "The magazine ran fast-action tales of suitably hard-nosed and hard-boiled detectives," comments pulp historian Will Murray. "Margulies liked to say that his line was 'probably the fastest bunch of all pulps.' This meant, quite simply, nonstop action, and action was what *Thrilling Detective* delivered—even if it was sometimes at the expense of characterization and, in keeping with the Great Depression trends, no continued stories." A couple of years later came *Popular Detective*, more or less the mixture as before, but costing a nickel more.

Nick Carter made a comeback in the thirties, this time taking on many of the characteristics of a hard-boiled private eye. The first issue of Street & Smith's *Nick Carter Magazine* was dated March 1933. The new pulp was a monthly, selling for ten cents. The Nick of these novels was still a supersleuth and beloved of the law—"a call and nineteen thousand policemen would be at his command." But he was much tougher, and far less gentlemanly, than in previous incarnations. When annoyed by the uncooperative girlfriend of a troublesome hophead:

"I'm tired of being waltzed around," Nick Carter snapped. You've got too many peculiar friends—" he mimicked the girl's cooing tones of a moment before—"Irma."

With a hoodlum who's annoying him he's equally tough:

> The man dipped for his gun.
> But Nick Carter's revolver was already in his hand, pointing at the crook.
> "There's no evidence against you," Nick Carter said. "You haven't done a thing, except make a little speech. So you can go, bad boy. But first"— Nick Carter stepped forward, flipped a gun out of the man's armpit, ran a practiced hand over the man's body—"first, I'll take your popgun away from you, and I'll go like this."
> The gun was an automatic. Nick shot the clip out of it, broke it open to eject the cartridge that had been in the chamber. He handed the gun back with exaggerated politeness.
> "You can take your little scent-sprinkler back to your boss now, and tell him I'll be seeing him in Room 1718, the Hotel Metropolitan. Scram, punk!"

Besides the increasing reader interest in tough detectives, Nick Carter owed his latest rebirth to the increasingly impressive sales of *The Shadow*, started in 1931. Street & Smith had been cautiously planning how best to succeed again with hero pulp titles. In 1933 came Doc Savage and Nick Carter. "In February W. H. Ralston had John Nanovic bring me into his august presence," Richard Wormser once explained to me. "The Shadow had been so successful that they were going to revive Nick Carter, who had been off the stands since about 1924. Could I write a novel every other week? Being young, ignorant, and hungry I said sure and became Nick Carter." Actually Wormser didn't have to write quite that much under the Carter pen name. "I wrote seventeen in ten months, however, and received a little less than five thousand dollars for a little more than a million words. That was good money for that lowest of twentieth-century years." The pulp continued without Wormser with lesser men taking over. Nick's pulp expired with its fortieth issue (June 1936). He didn't make it as a magazine hero in that hard-boiled decade, but he'd be back in movies, on radio, and in comic books.

When the Clayton magazine empire collapsed in 1933, several of its titles were bought up by rival publishers. Street & Smith picked up three—*Cowboy Stories*, *Astounding*, and *Clues*. The detective pulp, around since 1926, had been priced at twenty cents and then fifteen cents. During its heyday from 1928 to 1930, *Clues* was issued twice a month. S&S took charge with the issue dated October 1933, several months after the last Clayton issue. The price was soon dropped to ten cents. *Clues* had always been a politer sort of pulp, allowing writers like Erle Stanley Gardner into its pages but making certain they didn't act too tough. In the early thirties there was increasing emphasis on series characters, and in the mid-thirties a few more hard-boiled writers showed up, including Cleve F. Adams and T. T. Flynn. There were still quite a few exotic investigators on hand, though, such as E. Hoffmann Price's turbaned Pawang Ali, "the Sherlock Holmes of Singapore."

Anthony Rud, an author himself and former editor of *Adventure*, took over as editor of *Clues* in 1936. The magazine became somewhat less sedate during his three-year term there. Erle Stanley Gardner returned in 1938, after an absence of five years, with a series about a brash criminal lawyer named Barney Killigen. "I'm a great respecter of the law," Killigen explained, "but when the spirit of the law conflicts with the letter of the law, I'm a man of spirit rather than of letters." There were four novelets about him, narrated by his pretty secretary and demonstrating Killigen's unorthodox approach to the practice of law. While working on a case he was fond of placing want ads in the newspapers requesting such items as a mean-tempered skunk and a gaggle of bathing beauties. He'd drop in at the Plumbers' and Pipe Fitters' Annual Ball and manage to utilize all these odd people, places, and things to win his cases. Killigen was nearly always overdrawn at the bank, and he never passed up a chance to confiscate any loose cash he ran into during his investigations.

Race Williams showed up once in *Clues* in 1940. The Avenger, after his own pulp flopped, did five turns in 1942 and 1943. The magazine ceased in the autumn of 1943 with its 216th issue.

Tougher, funnier, and somewhat more audacious was Street & Smith's *Crime Busters*. Edited by John Nanovic, who was in charge of *The Shadow* and *Doc Savage*, it was intended as a showcase for detective characters who might prove appealing enough to be promoted into pulps of their own. To measure popularity, early issues included ballots with which readers were encouraged to vote for their favorites. Lester Dent contributed Click Rush the Gadget Man, and Theodore Tinsley created Carrie Cashin, a feisty lady P.I. From Walter Gibson, who claimed that the idea for this try-out pulp had been his, came Norgil the magician detective. W. T. Ballard wrote of Red Drake, a racetrack sleuth, and Frank Gruber cooked up Jim Strong, "one-man Racket Squad." The incomparable Norvell Page auditioned both Angus St. Cloud, alias the Death Angel, and private eye Dick Barrett. Barrett, who was as wacky as most of Page's other creations, specialized in crimes involving stolen gems. He operated out of a gimmick-laden office that provided some lively encounters:

> Barrett leaned forward sharply. "Then why try to play tricks on me, Miss Dean!" he said angrily. "You've still got the ruby!" He circled the desk, tapped her on the chest with an indignant finger. "You've got the ruby right between your breasts! Will you hand it over or—shall I take it!"
>
> The girl stared up at him. She was genuinely frightened now. "Why, how dare you—"
>
> Barrett said coldly, "Why try to lie? I know you have the ruby. All jewels are fluorescent under certain light rays. You're in line with a machine of my own design which focuses rays of varying lengths on your body. When I looked at you through the glass, I saw the glow of a ruby hung around your neck. I work for the insurance company, Miss Dean. You reported the ruby lost. Now, either turn it over, or I'll take it!"

Despite the popularity of the characters, especially Carrie Cashin, the Gadget Man, and Norgil, no new pulps featuring them were ever published, possibly because they were only popular with a relatively small readership. "You would think that readers would flock to a magazine with authors such as Maxwell Grant, Kenneth Robeson, Ted Tinsley, Steve Fisher, etc.," observed Nanovic many years later. "But the magazine just plodded along." *Crime Busters* changed its name to *Mystery* in 1939 and survived as such until 1943. Looking back on his pulp-editing career, Nanovic felt that his biggest disappointment was *Crime Busters*.

Another interesting, and unappreciated, magazine was *Double Detective*. This fifteen-cent monthly was edited by Preston Grady, published by the Munsey Company, and drew its contributors from the most popular writers of Munsey's other major pulps, *Argosy* and *Detective Fiction Weekly*. A statement in the first issue explained:

> Our title tells the policy in a nutshell. *Double Detective* is two complete magazines in one. First, as you can see on the opposite page, a big assortment of novelettes and short stories by the best detective writers we know. Also, in addition, a book-length mystery novel complete in each issue.

Included in the premier number were Cleve F. Adams, Richard Sale, Cornell Woolrich, Max Brand, Roger Torrey, and Leslie Charteris. The Saint, thanks to the enterprising Charteris, appeared in a number of different pulpwoods in the thirties and forties. The novel was by Dale Clark. Unlike what were passed off as complete novels in some pulps, those in *Double Detective* usually ran between 40,000 and 50,000 words.

Grady seems to have encouraged several writers to attempt longer works. Notable among them were John K. Butler and Norbert Davis, both excellent writers who never received sufficient recognition. Butler wrote several novels and short novels for *Double Dectective*, something he did for no other magazine. Davis, too, turned out lengthier stuff. He did both a novel, *Murder on the Mississippi*, and a novelet, "Death of a Medicine Man," about a struggling young lawyer who gets involved with murders in a small rural town on the banks of the Mississippi. Much gloomier, and with hardly any of Davis's characteristic humor, was a novel entitled *String Him Up* (February 1938). A bleak story about an outcast D.A. who fights his way back, it uses the hobo jungles of the Depression and a corrupt California town as settings. Almost a decade later, after a minimal revision by W. T. Ballard, this novel was published in hard cover under the title *Murder Picks the Jury*. The joint pen name was Harrison Hunt.

Editorials played up the notion that this was also a magazine of recurring detectives. Readers' opinions were solicited: "How often do you like a series character to appear? Which ones are your favorites? Just drop us a card telling your preferences and we'll do the rest." By 1939 the number of repeat appearances had increased. Frequently seen were Cleve F. Adams's Lieutenant John J. Shannon, Walter Ripperger's Carter DeRaven, and Richard Sale's Calamity Quade—"the papers call him Calamity Quade because something calamitous happens when he takes a case."

The April 1940 issue saw the advent of yet another series character, this one signaling a change in policy. The Green Lama was to have the full-length novel to himself from now on. He represented an attempt by the now faltering Munsey Company to beef up sales by offering the public another Shadow simulacrum. That kept *Double Detective* going, eventually as a shaky bimonthly, until early in 1943.

With *Detective Tales* Popular Publications intended a magazine that would avoid series characters while concentrating on "detective stories with a punch!" The first issue was dated August 1935 and its opening statement was aimed at customers who might already be suffering from an overdose of tough-guy private eyes. After evoking the shade of O. Henry, the editors went on to say:

> O. Henry wrote of crime—but he seldom wasted precious words on the dry-as-dust business of questioning stupid witnesses and hunting—through endless pages—for clues that mean little or nothing when found. Not all of his detectives were hard-boiled automatons, with neither human feeling nor good sense. He wrote about real people—and the reader suffered and rejoiced with them, in direct proportion with their reality—with their humanity!
>
> It is the aim of Detective Tales to bring back some of that humanity and breathless drama and soul-stirring emotion to the art of detective story writing. And because we believe that a good detective story is usually a short one—because we stand firmly convinced that the people of America like their fiction terse and dramatic, human, and straight from the shoulder—we are able to crowd into these pages of this magazine more real value and more stories than we believe has ever been attempted in any periodical.

That turned out to be the twelve stories for ten cents that so many of their competitors would be striving for. The actual stories—by the likes of Frederick C. Davis, Norvell Page, Wyatt Blassingame, and Paul Ernst—were less like O. Henry and more like the sort of thing found in most of the other tough-detective pulps, wedged in among the series stories. Henry Steeger provided the usual surefire Popular packaging—a cover painting by Walter Baumhofer depicting big trouble in a Chinatown den, with plenty of red, yellow, and black. Interior illustrations were by Ralph Carlson and Paul Orban, two of the better pulp artists. For customers who were fonder of the Yellow Peril than of O. Henry, *Detective Tales* offered frequent covers, some by Baumhofer and others by Tom Lovell, featuring variations on the theme of stalwart gun-toting detective and damsel in distress coping with wily Oriental assaults.

Detective Tales proved to be a sturdy periodical, surviving until 1953. It underwent, of course, several changes of policy. "It began with wild action-melodrama and ended in modernized hard-boiled stories of relentless movement," observes Robert Sampson. "Between those two points, the magazine published mystery-action fiction in all its variety, from suspense to atmospheric terror, from deduction to wild, gun, free-for-alls. . . . It was a colorful, urgent, vigorous periodical, foaming with cheerful excesses; it was one of the classic pulp magazines."

Chapter 6

The New Wild West

It was in the blurb he wrote to introduce the initial installment of "Fast One" that Joseph Shaw first referred to Los Angeles and Hollywood as "the New Wild West." That was in the March 1932 issue and by then *Black Mask* had already been running hard-boiled stories with Southern California settings for well over a year. Of course, it wasn't cowboys shooting it out with owlhoots anymore. In the New Wild West you found private detectives going up against gangsters, gamblers, and crooked cops, all of it taking place in a sun-drenched, slightly surrealistic landscape where newly rich movie people mingled with newly rich criminals while old money millionaires and corrupt politicians looked on.

The real Los Angeles was not a very honest, nor a very fragrant, place in the thirties. *Corrupt* is the word historians most frequently apply to the public officials who ran things and to the moneyed elite who controlled things from behind the scenes. "Through most of the Twenties and Thirties, the city was controlled by a group of men known locally as the Combination," report Christopher Finch and Linda Rosenkrantz in *Gone Hollywood*, "who paid off law-enforcement agencies and provided protection for a variety of illegal activities, from gambling to prostitution, in return for fiscal tributes said to amount to $50 million a year." L.A. Mayor Frank Shaw was recalled in the early 1930s, and the head of the LAPD, James "Two Gun" Davis, was fired in 1939 after his chief of detectives was convicted of attempted murder.

Like oranges and movies, organized crime thrived in the salutary climate. Gambling was especially lucrative, and from 1929 on, one of the favorite spots for it was aboard the casino ships anchored beyond the three-mile limit off Long Beach and Santa Monica. The most popular of these was the *Rex*. "Equipped to accommodate more than 3,000 gamblers at a time," reported John Ross Babcock in *L.A. Style* magazine, "the *Rex* had a dining capacity of 500. Its gambling facilities included 300 slot machines as well as crap and roulette tables, off-track betting and even a faro wheel. Water taxis left the Santa Monica Pier every 15 minutes."

Gangsters were frequently to be seen mixing with the notables of both Los Angeles and cinema society. Jack Dragna was the local Mafia rep, but easterners such as Longie Zwillman, who allegedly romanced platinum-haired Jean Harlow, and Bugsy Siegel relocated in the L.A. area. Siegel, a friend of Jimmy Durante, George Raft, Jack Warner, and Louis B. Mayer, was a welcome guest at social functions and such fashionable night spots as Ciro's and Romanoff's. Another of Bugsy's lady friends was actress Wendy Barrie, who on the screen portrayed the lady friend of both the Saint and the Falcon.

The links between the movie business and organized crime were many. For a time two transplanted Chicago hoods, Willie Bioff and George Browne, controlled the International Alliance of Theatrical Stage Employees and Moving Picture Operators. They were able to extort annual sums ranging from $25,000 to $100,000 from studios to guarantee there'd be no crippling strikes of movie projectionists. Movie studios also often provided the raw material for the thriving prostitution racket. "For some of the girls, whose best performances for an influential studio affiliate may have been on the casting couch, it was a relatively short step to fame and fortune," point out Zelda Cini and Bob Crane in *Hollywood: Land and Legend*. "Others found it both expedient and profitable to stick with the casting couch, so to speak. As a matter of fact, some of the best brothels in Hollywood and Los Angeles were owned and operated, *in absentia*, of course, by studio executives."

Hammett brought the private eye westward, to San Francisco and the smaller cities and towns of Northern California. Raoul Whitfield had his private eye set up shop in Southern California. His "Death in a Bowl" is the very first Hollywood private-detective novel and it remains one of the best. *Black Mask* ran the book as a three-part serial from September through November 1930. Whitfield's detective is Ben Jardinn: "He had dark eyes and hair. His body was lean, but it had firmness. He was in his late thirties. His voice was soft; when he spoke he had a habit of turning his head away from the person to whom he talked." Jardinn and his partner, Max Cohn, whom he doesn't trust, do business out of an office "in a frame building two blocks from Grauman's Chinese Theatre." He's romantically interested in his secretary, Carol Torney, but he doesn't trust her, either. In fact, Jardinn trusts nobody. "Money will buy almost anything—in Hollywood," he says early on. And he later observes, "So many humans tell lies. It's hell finding out what really happens." Although he's accused of being cold and hard-boiled, Jardinn is actually compassionate and concerned. "The reader knows that this toughness," suggests Carolyn See in an essay on the Hollywood novel, "is only appearance, an individual's defense against an intolerably meaningless world."

The "Bowl" of the title is the Hollywood Bowl and it's there that the first killing takes place. It's a flamboyant murder, with the orchestra conductor gunned down as he directs in the open-air theater. The maestro is the brother of one of Jardinn's clients, who is on the scene when the shooting takes place. Even so, it takes Jardinn awhile to find out who did it. The concrete band shell that everyone associates with the Hollywood Bowl wasn't built until 1929, and Whitfield was probably the first to use it as a fictional setting.

The story is told in a knowing, matter-of-fact style. Whitfield plays it close to the vest, concentrating on what his characters say and do and using Hollywood as a backdrop, a series of sets in which his story unfolds. Were this filmed as written, there would be more close-ups and two-shots than long shots. Unlike some who followed, Whitfield never waxed lyrical and he evoked the look and feel of Los Angeles with terse, underplayed descriptions:

> It was ten after eight when Jardinn turned off Hollywood Boulevard to the right, moved up Highland to the Bowl.

* * *

It was almost two in the morning. Jardinn got up and shoved the window wide. There was nothing on Hollywood Boulevard but street car tracks and sidewalks.

Many of what became the standard props of the Hollywood private-eye novel are to be found in "Death in a Bowl," such as the cocky cynicism and the hard-boiled pragmatism. Chided by one of his clients for playing both sides against the middle, Jardinn responds grimly, "I'm after a killer—man or woman. It's my business. I'll take your money and Ernst Reiner's money. I'll take anyone's money, if I can give something for it. This isn't a hobby with me." A new secretary who asks if she's likely to be hurt while working for him is told, "Don't kid yourself—you won't get hurt. You may get killed, but it'll be so sudden there won't be pain."

There is also a preoccupation with the unreality and artificiality of people and things. For instance, Jardinn tells a young woman he feels is trying to con him, "Come out of it. There're enough actresses in this hokum town as it is." When a suspect asks him, "Do I look like a killer?" Jardinn answers, "I never saw a man who looked like one. You look like a liar to me—I've seen them before."

Whitfield's private eye also gets the opportunity to drop in at the homes of the rich and famous, such as leading actress Myra Rand, who "sat across from him, gracefully indolent in the huge, fan-backed chair. She wore a jet black evening gown—white pearls in a long string contrasted the color. Her skin was beautiful; with no harsh, studio lights to strike her she was a gorgeous thing." There are as well glimpses of sound stages, night spots, and a variety of

Hollywood types. Jardinn's reaction to an encounter with Long, a brash movie songwriter, sums up his attitude to the whole place: "He decided that Long and Hollywood were well mated; both were noisy and colorful. And clever."

The footloose Whitfield first hit Hollywood before World War I, approximately at the time the town was starting to think about becoming the movie capital of the world. "Acted in motion pictures," he admitted in a later memoir, "and survived." He returned to Hollywood for a while in the late 1920s. According to an autobiographical note he wrote in 1931, he was probably no longer in Southern California when he did the actual writing of "Death in a Bowl." He said, "Have been writing in New York, Paris, Switzerland, Italy and Tudor City in the past year." He was apparently back in L.A. in 1933, since he uses the severe earthquake that shook the area in March of that year in "Dark Death" (*Black Mask*, August 1933). This was one of a pair of short stories that he did about Jardinn; the other was "Murder by Request" (*Black Mask*, January 1933). Nineteen thirty-three is also the year Warner Brothers released *Private Detective 62*, which was based on an original story by Whitfield. Directed by Michael Curtiz, who is best remembered for *Casablanca*, it starred William Powell and Margaret Lindsay.

Whitfield's single private-eye story for *Argosy* also dealt with a Hollywood operative. "Cruise to Nowhere" ran in the December 23, 1933, issue of the fiction weekly and was a decidedly unseasonal novelet about a gambling ship anchored off Long Beach, a movie actress in trouble, and a kidnaping conspiracy involving a collaboration between gangsters and a studio executive. It featured Ben Casey, a wisecracking transplanted New Yorker who is brash, aggressive, and unimpressed by either the criminal or the motion picture elite. During a shipboard search for the missing movie star this exchange takes place between him and a gent who may or may not be a fellow op:

"Hello," Sands hailed. "Find her?"

Ben Casey nodded. "I've got her locked in my cabin, with a few other stars who have been using this boat. She felt faint, knocked over some chairs in her cabin and upset the desk; she stuck her head out of the port and then fell over. Luckily there was a rope dangling from the stern. She grabbed it and hung on. I heard her feeble cries and hauled her up."

Sands said, "Uh-huh. How about the note?"

Casey grinned. "She doesn't remember about that."

Sands said, "Uh-huh. How about the other stars?"

"They were hanging on to the rope, too. They fell over on previous trips, but as they weren't working in any pictures their public didn't miss them. Their husbands didn't care, anyway."

Sands said, "Seriously—I've been all over the boat and I haven't spotted Joan Lansing."

Ben Casey whistled softly. "Did you look in the engine room?" he asked. "I read in a fan magazine that Joan just loved the engines on big boats, and that she'd always wanted to be a stoker."

Just after Whitfield introduced Ben Jardinn, Fred Mac-Isaac began a series of cynical, satirical stories about crime and intrigue in the movie capital for *Argosy*. His central character was not a detective, though, but a brash press agent with the unmelodic name of Bill Peepe. MacIsaac, a large red-haired man in his forties, was living in Hollywood at the time "on top of Lookout Mountain which is higher than the Empire State Building and from which an even finer view is obtained." A former newspaper reporter and drama critic, he had firsthand knowledge of the ways of publicity men and show business in general. The initial adventure of the amiable, opportunistic Peepe was entitled "The British Blonde" and appeared in the December 13, 1930, issue of the Munsey weekly.

Peepe, who married the rising young movie actress he met in the initial story, was "not an estimable person. He had so many faults it would take hours to detail them. He was unprincipled, shifty and unable to resist strong drink very long." He also had a tendency to stray if any other lovely picture stars smiled at him alluringly—"Bill loved his wife but she was away on location." Peepe encountered kidnaping, con games, and crooked gambling in the course of his career as he strived to pull off his schemes and live well off his wife's money. The stories were filled with effective descriptions of Hollywood during the final years of Prohibition:

> Mr. William Peepe stirred, grunted, groaned and sat up. He was lying in his big bed in his chamber in his castle on top of Lookout Mountain. From the huge window opposite the foot of the bed he had a magnificent view of the Pacific Ocean with the peak of Catalina Island, fifty miles away, in the distance.

So clear was the day that he almost could have seen William Wrigley, the chewing gum king, who owns Catalina Island, sitting on top of the peak, but Mr. Peepe couldn't see very well on account of the pain in both eyes. Furthermore he had been afflicted in his sleep by some fantastic disease which caused his head to swell to four times its normal size.

There are no sidewalks upon the road down from the mountain and pedestrians are not considered at all, which is right and proper because there are no pedestrians. Nobody who didn't drive a car would dream of going up or down that road.

On Sunset Boulevard in Los Angeles is an imposing mansion set in the center of spacious grounds. Its inhabitants are so retiring that the old ladies from Iowa living in neighboring apartment houses or bungalows who sit at their windows by the hour hopeful of excitement have remarked that they must be very quiet and refined.

The old ladies retire about nine in the evening, however, and by eleven, Hollywood resembles the deserted village that Goldsmith wrote about. So the persons who get out of automobiles and pass through the gate and up the walk to the sedate mansion are never observed.

What these ladies have as a neighbor is an illegal gambling joint.

Although frequently a coward, Peepe could be as tough as any P.I. if need be. In rescuing his wife from gangsters, for instance:

> Now he saw a flight of stairs and descending the stairs, gun in hand, was Dink Spavoni.
>
> Bill Peepe saw red. He thrust both his weapons against the window frame and began firing with both hands. One of six or eight wild bullets passed through the body of Dink Spavoni. He lurched and fell headlong down a half dozen steps.
>
> Tearing open the front door, Bill Peepe, both revolvers held in his left hand, rushed into the room which was a shambles. He leaped over the body of Dink Spavoni and ran up the stairs, gun in each hand again.

Another Hollywood dick who knew his way around was Mark Hull, a former stuntman who became an opportunistic private eye after an accident fouled up his career. He appeared exactly once, in Norbert Davis's "Kansas City Flash" (*Black Mask*, March 1933). Davis knew Southern California well, as only a transplanted midwesterner can. And like his detective, "he was a cynically tolerant spectator of the flea circus that is Hollywood." The story deals with the kidnaping of an important actress, and when Hull calls at her studio to see how much they'll pay him to bring her back alive, he walks through that juxtaposition of the real and the fake that was to figure in so many later Hollywood detective yarns:

He walked down the corridor and out another door into the sunlight. He followed a cement walk through a small lawn and was in a narrow street flanked on each side by two-story, barn-like buildings with corrugated iron doors.

There were some cowboys sitting around in the shade, smoking and talking in low tones. They looked hot and tired. A soldier went by, dragging his rifle behind him, his hob-nails clanking on the cement. Two girls in evening dresses followed him. In a doorway three men in horn-rimmed glasses were arguing earnestly. A supervisor went by, walking alone and talking to himself.

Davis, in what he wrote for the less restrictive markets such as *Black Mask* and *Dime Detective*, always blended comedy and toughness. And, again like his op, "he appeared to be hard-boiled and good-humored at the same time." The dialogue is laced with wisecracks, but there is a tough, sometimes slow-motion violence as well:

Mark Hull let the fist go. The other went head-first over the couch into the corner behind it. His short, crooked legs stayed in sight for an instant, then slid limply downward.

Mark Hull dragged him from under the couch and plopped him down on the cushions. He sat there and stared vacantly ahead with his big mouth twitching loosely. Mark Hull scraped a chair over and sat down facing the couch. He took a .38 Colt automatic from his shoulder-holster.

Consciousness suddenly flicked back into the greasy one's eyes.

"Police b——!" he said.

"I'm not from the police. I'm from the studio. We're going to play this game until you tell me where your new hideout is."

"Go to hell!"

Mark Hull cracked him again.

The next year Davis sold two more Hollywood tales to *BM*, both about Ben Shaley:

> Shaley was bonily tall. He had a thin, tanned face with bitterly heavy lines in it. He looked calm; but he looked like he was being calm on purpose—as though he was consciously holding himself in. He had an air of hardboiled confidence.

In "Red Goose" (February 1934) he's hired to find a stolen painting. Davis makes use of some typical 1930s Los Angeles settings:

> Hingle Manor was a long, neat two-story stucco building with turrets on the four corners and blue pennants on each of the turrets. Floodlights placed on the front lawn and slanted up made the building look larger and newer than it was.

When a blonde who can't be as naive and innocent as she seems tries to sell him back the missing masterpiece, he is somewhat skeptical:

Shaley grunted. He scratched his head, scowling.
He said:

"Listen, Marjorie, I'm just a nasty man with
mean suspicions. The only kind of fairy stories I
believe are the kind they tell about the boys who
carry handkerchiefs in their cuffs. Just sit right
here while I sniff around."

Davis, who was in his mid-twenties then, was already
good at describing violence and action:

Shaley's coat ripped, and he went backward. He
bounced off the table, fell over a chair. He got up
quickly. He was breathing in gasping sobs. Over
Gorjon's shoulder he caught a quick glimpse of
the rest of the room and realized that all this was
happening in seconds instead of hours.

Tannerwell was still shaking Carter by the
neck. Carter's plump face was beginning to turn
purple. He was trying to get a revolver from his
pocket, but apparently the sight had caught in the
cloth and, with Tannerwell shaking him, he
couldn't get it free.

Marjorie Smith was still sitting on the couch.
And she was laughing. She was laughing at
Carter, pointing her finger mockingly at him.

Shaley's second case was "The Price of a Dime" (April
1934). This one involved him with murder and the movies.
The studio is not that impressive a place this time:

The high board fence had once been painted a
very bright shade of yellow, but now the paint was

old and faded and streaked. It was peeling off in big patches that showed bare, brown board underneath.

Shaley parked his battered Chrysler roadster around the corner and walked back along the fence. There was a group of Indians standing in a silent, motionless circle in front of the big iron gate. They all had their arms folded across their chests. They all wore gaudy shirts, and two of the older ones had strips of buckskin with beads sewn on them tied around their heads.

They didn't look at Shaley, didn't pay any attention to him.

The violence remains first-rate:

A fat man in a pink shirt was sitting in an old rocker on the porch with his feet up on the railing.

"Where's Bennie Smith's room?" Shaley asked him abruptly.

"Who?"

"Bennie Smith?"

"What's his name?" the fat man inquired innocently.

Shaley hooked the toe of his right foot under the fat man's legs and heaved up. The fat man gave a frightened squawk and went over backwards, chair and all. He rolled over and got up on his hands and knees, gaping blankly at Shaley.

Shaley leaned over him. "Where's Bennie Smith's room?"

In 1936, for *Detective Fiction Weekly*, Davis turned out a series about an investigator named Simeon Saxon, who operated out of a corrupt town named Bay City. (Raymond Chandler didn't invent Bay City. He, as did Davis, simply called Santa Monica by its long-held nickname.) *DFW* seems to have inhibited Davis a bit, and most of the many stories he did for the magazine are somewhat subdued, with less wisecracking and less quirky violence. Saxon worked among the less affluent segments of Southern Cal society and there are plenty of mean streets, cheap hotels, all-night drugstores, and small cafés:

> The Blue Light Café was on Burr Street just off East Fifth Avenue, in the heavy commercial district of Bay City. The buildings in this area were squat, smoke-grimed, old. The pavement on the street had been riddled and roughened by the constant pound of heavy trucks over a period of years.
>
> The café was in the middle of a block. It had been a speakeasy in the days of prohibition. It was flush with the street, and there was no name displayed. There was none needed. The place had a reputation.

Usually Davis managed to get in some violent action:

> All in one lithely smooth motion Pinta whipped around and hurled the knife in a flatly glittering arc straight at Saxon's chest. Rose Graham gave a gulping little cry of terror.
>
> Saxon stepped back a little, moving the kitchen

door in front of him. The knife blade thudded hard into the wood. Saxon jumped forward again, swinging the automatic up.

Pinta swung away from him, snarling. He tripped over a chair, stumbled. In that split-second, while he was off balance, Saxon swung the automatic down, smashing Pinta over the temple with the butt.

Pinta went head first into the couch, bounced limply off on to the floor. He sprawled out laxly there, face down. Saxon stood over him, watching warily.

Bill Lennox had most of the attributes of a Hollywood P.I. He was tough and cynical and could get sentimental over a girl in trouble. He was an insider, though, an employee of a large studio run by a gent named Sol Spurck:

Bill Lennox, trouble-shooter for General-Consolidated Studio, walked through the outer office. Trouble-shooter wasn't his title. In fact, one of the things which Lennox lacked was an official title. Those in Hollywood who didn't like him, called him Spurck's watch-dog. Ex-reporter, ex-publicity man, he had drifted into his present place through his inability to say yes and his decided ability in saying no.

W. T. Ballard's Lennox stories ran in *Black Mask* from 1933 to 1942, providing a good picture of what life was like on the other side of studio walls. That life included a good deal of intrigue, double-dealing, and, fairly often, murder.

Another transplanted midwesterner, Ballard was an ex-reporter himself and had worked as a writer for Warner and Columbia. He'd also sold to the pulps. When I was gathering material for *Cheap Thrills*, back in the late 1960s, he wrote me an account of how he had come to create his troubleshooter:

> I was helping to produce six cheap Westerns, when I came home one night to find the radio on and a trailer advertising *The Maltese Falcon* running. I listened to it. It was the type of stuff that I had wanted to write, but the detective pulps of the period were using mostly the puzzle story. Anyhow the picture was playing Warner Brothers. I went downtown and caught it. The credits mentioned *Black Mask* of which I had never heard.
>
> When the show was over, I went to the Owl drug store and bought a copy of *Black Mask*, which I read on the street car going home. The story that attracted me most was one by Ted Tinsley about a New York columnist. I thought it over, at first thinking to do a Hollywood columnist. But that was pretty close. Then I thought of Lawson, a friend of mine in the foreign department at Universal who the Laemmle family used as an errand boy to keep the kid out of trouble.
>
> So, I'd do a Hollywood Trouble Shooter. I couldn't use the name Lawson, but I liked the sound. So I went to the phone book and ran down the list until I came to the name Lennox.
>
> At midnight I sat down and began to write. At

eight o'clock the following morning I finished the
ten thousand word novelette and mailed it on my
way to the office. A week later I had an air mail
from Shaw saying he liked the story, that he
wanted a page change at the end and enclosed the
check for two hundred bucks since he did not
want to hold me up. No editor had ever done
anything like that before and from then on he was
my boy.

I sat down and wrote him another story that
night. I sold him six in seven weeks. Then he
wrote that Phil Cody, who was still serving as the
business manager, thought that they'd better hold
off buying any more for about three or four
months.

In the whole time I worked for Shaw he never
rejected a story.

Other writers made use of troubleshooters, notably Erle
Stanley Gardner. His Jax Keen worked for a movie studio
run by Abie Blitzmount, and two novelets about him were
featured in *Double Detective* (November 1939 and February 1940). Keen narrated his own tales, which dealt with
blackmail, murder, and the other usual troubles of the
motion picture industry. He was tough, jaded, and quite a
bit more cynical than Lennox:

The glamour personalities of the screen, eh? They
may be glamour to you. They're a pain in the neck
to me.

You see the buildup by hundreds of expensive
publicity writers. I see the real thing. You read in

the movie magazines that Sally Silly faced the heartache which came into her life with a dry-eyed bravery that pulls the heartstrings—about how John Mushface, driving to the studio for a late appointment, saw a baby kitten in the road too late to stop. He swerved his car to avoid hitting the kitten and crashed into the rear end of a truck. He cheerfully paid all damages and said simply, "I have always liked kittens."

That's the story you get.

They call me out of bed at three o'clock in the morning because John Mushface got pickled and tried to drive home. He mistook the rear end of a truck for his garage driveway. It's up to me to think up the kitten angle and go out and find some kitten for the newspaper photographers to get busy on when they write the story from a sob sister angle.

And as far as Sally Silly is concerned—be your age, brother. Be your age.

John K. Butler was born in California and grew up in Auburn, a small town north of Sacramento. He moved to Southern California in the late 1920s, after getting hired as a reader at Universal. In an autobiographical piece written for the *American Fiction Guild Bulletin* in 1935, he told his colleagues:

Sooner or later Hollywood enters the life of every writer. The routine is that you begin by writing plays, books, criticisms, magazine stuff, poems, or obituaries, practically anything except

> movie scripts, and then some producer gets a
> momentary idea he can't make a picture without
> you. So you trek westward to be disillusioned. I
> seem to be reversing the routine. Got my disillu-
> sioning first. Started work in a flicker-factory some
> years ago. Was on the editorial staff of several
> studios. Had my fling at penning scenarios—
> which is one experience I can't crowd into this
> thumbnail. Get me tight some night and learn
> why.

Despite his Hollywood experience, Butler wrote very little about studio life. He was interested in the whole of his native state, setting stories in San Francisco, Los Angeles, and even Watsonville. He started selling to *Black Mask* and *Dime Detective* in 1935. His first series for *Dime Detective* dealt with Rex Lonergan, a hard-boiled Frisco cop. Next came Tricky Enright, also in *Dime Detective*, who was an undercover man for the governor's office and thought to be a crook by most cops:

> My criminal reputation is just a blind to cover my
> real work as undercover operator working direct-
> ly out of the Governor's office. My salary comes
> from a Secret Service fund alloted each year to
> the State Attorney General for private investiga-
> tions, and my name isn't entered on any payroll
> list. In fact, no records are kept at all, because my
> life as well as my job depends on absolute secrecy.

The six Enright stories are tough, well constructed, and filled with the look and feel of California in the thirties:

I stood on a corner in the town. It was a windlessly cold night. Beyond the town, the Sierra Nevada Mountains rose straight up to their highest peaks. There was snow up there. Even though no breezes came down into the valley, I could feel the chill breath of snow. In the valley, the snow didn't fall, but there was a bitter, dry cold that settled down from the high altitudes into the orange-groves.

The growers had begun to "smudge."

For miles and miles, through the valley groves, the smudge-pots burned. Laborers, mostly Mexican, plodded over plowed ground, tending the oil fires that burned, in pots under each tree, to ward off frost.

Thick smoke, from the night's smudging, rose heavily into the sharp, cold atmosphere and made a black fog over everything. People shut their windows against it, but the smudge-smoke crept through cracks, seeped under doors, settled into furniture and curtains.

Marine Street ran through the cheapest, honky-tonk part of town. It was narrow, almost an alley, and the crowded dirty buildings had been remodeled to resemble the architecture of Venice, Italy. Many plaster ornaments had cracked or fallen, and a building which had once been a respectable hotel was now a beer-parlor downstairs and a penny dance-hall above.

Butler created an assortment of private eyes and cops, doing novelets and short stories for such pulps as

Detective Fiction Weekly and *Double Detective*. His best, and final, series ran in *Dime Detective* from 1940 to 1942. Steve Midnight was a cabdriver—"the hardluck hacker," blurbs called him. He was a former playboy down on his luck, and the nine novelets about him are all excellent examples of the hard-boiled first-person Hollywood detective story. Steven Middleton Knight first acquired his nickname back in his all-night carousing period, but it was equally applicable to him as the driver of an all-night taxi. He always had, as David Geherin points out in *The American Private Eye*, the strongest of motives for taking on a case, either to collect on a fare he'd been stiffed out of or to extricate himself from a mess with the police. "His involvement in most cases is prompted by personal motives," says Geherin. "He has no professional interest in a case, either as a defender of justice or as someone hired by a client, nor does he meddle in police affairs as a whim." Geherin also points out that, as a writer,

> Butler possessed two notable qualities: first, he was adept at developing a plot well, unfolding his mystery with sure pacing while also allowing for excellent character development; second, he paid careful attention to details, both in the creation of his characters and in the description of his settings. Like Raymond Chandler, he wrote about Los Angeles . . . and his stories provide a vivid sense of place.

A compassionate man, Steve Midnight often found himself starting to care about the people he met in his investigations. It was sometimes difficult for him to remain,

as an ideal private investigator is supposed to, nothing
more than a catalyst. He kept getting affected by what was
happening to him. "Dead Man's Alibi" (July 1941) con-
cludes with the suicide of the killer, who happens to be a
test pilot. Earlier Midnight had talked to a crippled
husband whose wife is far from faithful. The last lines are:

> The sound of the crash, ripping the earth apart,
> the sight of it exploding like a bomb of fire at the
> north end of Lockwood's testing field, would be
> with me for the rest of my life. I'd hear it and see
> it, day and night. It would wake me from vivid
> dreams with the shock of its reality.
>
> But I didn't dream of crashes that night. I
> dreamt about a lonely tired man who lived a life
> in a wheel-chair and waited for his wayward wife
> to come home.

Butler, a fugitive from the scenario departments, eventually, perhaps inevitably, went back to writing screenplays.
Dropping out of the pulps in the 1940s, he worked mostly
for Republic. He did a few mysteries, but the majority of
his scripts were westerns for such cowboy stars as Roy
Rogers, Gene Autry, Bob Steele, Don "Red" Barry, and
Wild Bill Elliott. He died in the mid-1960s. No books by
him were ever published, and with the exception of the
Steve Midnight story "The Saint in Silver," which was
reprinted in *The Hardboiled Dicks* in 1965, the only source
of his work remains the pulp magazines themselves.
"Because his stories never enjoyed hardcover publication,"
says Geherin, "Butler has been relegated to obscurity,
another of those writers who turned out consistently high

quality work yet who, thanks to the vagaries of the public market, is known only to devoted pulp collectors."

Many writers migrated westward in the thirties and forties, hoping to have luck in the movies. A few of them succeeded; most didn't. But quite a few of them, the successful ones and the others, wrote Hollywood mystery stories for the pulp markets. Among them were Frank Gruber, Dwight V. Babcock, Steve Fisher, Eric Taylor, Dale Clark, and Roger Torrey.

The Hollywood private eye survived the collapse of the pulps in the 1950s. By that time he'd branched out into hard covers and paperbacks and radio. L.A.-based ops like Philip Marlowe, Richard Diamond, and Jeff Regan all flourished over the airwaves. The private eye next jumped to television, where most of the conventions established over a half century ago in the pulps can still be observed.

Chapter 7

Dan Turner and the Spicy Gang

If she were willing to kick through with five grand—and other considerations—I'd play ball with her. I'm not in business for my health. Mine isn't a healthy business. I'm trying to accumulate enough coin to retire on before they start measuring my six feet three for a plush-lined coffin.

—*Dan Turner*

With the exception of the boys from *Black Mask*, most of the pulpwood private eyes hung out in magazines that sold for ten or fifteen cents. Dan Turner, the Hollywood gumshoe, was a two-bit detective, and to follow his slam-bang adventures in the thirties and forties you had to fork over a quarter. That was just one of his many distinctions. Turner appeared in more stories than any other pulp detective, he was featured in three separate magazines, and he was the only hard-boiled eye ever to have a magazine devoted exclusively to his exploits. Furthermore, he was one of the few pulp detectives ever to be written about in the slick pages of *The New Yorker*. And by the late 1930s Dan Turner and his Spicy cohorts were sharing office space with such rising heroes as Superman and Batman.

It all began in 1934 with *Spicy Detective Stories*, the twenty-five-cent pulp that was the flagship of a line that included *Spicy Adventure Stories* and *Spicy Mystery Stories*. Dan Turner, who quickly became the star of *Spicy*

Detective, wasn't even in Vol. 1, No. 1 (April 1934). His creator, Robert Leslie Bellem, was represented, however, by a third-person private-eye yarn. "The Shanghai Jester" was a fair example of the magazine's typical story, a blend of mystery puzzle, hard-boiled trappings, and the sort of humid approach to sex found in works labeled breezy or snappy. The opening is squarely in the tough fashion:

> Cliff Downey, ace operative of the Consolidated Detective Agency, strode down the thick-carpeted hallway of the fifth floor of the Hotel Cosmopole in Shanghai on the heels of a soft-footed Cantonese bell-hop.
>
> Cliff's hairy right fist was thrust deep into the pocket of his coat, the capable fingers clenched around the butt of a service .38 automatic.

But fairly soon Bellem's tale parted company with the sort of fare to be found in *Dime Detective* or *Black Mask*:

> The girl sat down beside him on the bed. With an abrupt gesture she tossed aside the robe from her snowy, perfect body. "Please say you like me just a little, Mr. Downey—Cliff!"
>
> She found his hand and pulled it around her warm, pliantly-bare waist. Involuntarily he found his fingers creeping upward along her velvet-smooth torso. He cupped her bare breast in his hand, and the thrill of the contact coursed along his arm like a warm flood. With a sudden savagery he turned and crushed her against his body, straining her backward with his ardor.

Despite his ardor, Downey wasn't the sort of P.I. to start a stampede to the newsstand. Nor were any of the other sleuths in that premier issue.

The second issue (June 1934) contained Bellem's "Murder by Proxy," in which Movieland's Supersleuth was introduced. Dan Turner was a nonpareil and the scores of stories Bellem cranked out about him constitute a great goofy saga. He was, as Bill Pronzini has said, "unlike any other detective invented for the pulp magazines, or for any other medium." Pronzini attributes much of Turner's popularity to "Bellem's breezy, sexy, colloquial style and the wildly improbable but at the same time completely predictable plots he concocted." Stephen Mertz, writing in *Twentieth Century Crime and Mystery Writers*, remarks that the Turner series "provided Bellem with an ongoing vehicle for constantly twisting fresh irreverent, funny angles out of the Hammett/Chandler tradition."

A few sourpuss critics have accused Bellem of being an unconscious humorist, claiming that the wild first-person prose of his Hollywood narratives was meant to be serious and simply misfired. Having read quite a few of the straight stories Bellem produced, under his own name and various aliases, I can testify that he was definitely kidding with Dan Turner. His straight stuff doesn't provoke unintended laughs and is, as a matter of fact, pretty average. His major achievement was the surrealistically colloquial style he worked out for these cockeyed tales of crime and passion in Southern California.

The style is what initially hooks readers. All the stories in *Spicy Detective* offered a certain amount of titillation. But only Bellem could open a story with "It startled the bejabbers out of me when the cute little blonde wren ankled into my apartment that evening and began stripping out of her threads." As Will Murray points out, "the minute your eyes skated across the opening paragraph of a Dan Turner yarn, perhaps against your better judgement, you were dragged into the story." What Bellam managed to do was create a real and distinct person. It's likely you'd go to some length to avoid a real-life counterpart of Dan Turner, but reading about him can be considerable fun.

The majority of Turner's cases revolved around movie people—actresses, actors, agents, directors, moguls—and such crimes as blackmail, theft, kidnaping, and murder. Bellem concentrated on characters and action, using Los Angeles as a backdrop rather than as an integral part of the story. "Bellem's evocation of the Hollywood milieu of the period," says Pronzini, "lacks the color and insights of Raymond Chandler, Steve Fisher and others who made Southern California their stock-in-trade." Bellem had lived in the L.A. area since the late 1920s and had worked as a newspaper reporter, radio announcer, and movie extra. So he actually knew this area as well as Chandler did, if not better. Yet he never bothered to re-create it in anything but a perfunctory way. Chandler builds his sets before our eyes, dresses them, and then unfolds his story. To Bellem all of L.A. was already there, a series of standing sets. Turner will mention a street or a place. If you see it in your mind's eye, fine; if not, no matter:

We'd just had supper at the Russian Emblem, on Vine.

I was cruising along Wilshire Boulevard, not thinking about anything in particular.

* * *

I was having a midnight snack at the Cocoanut Grove when Stan Sugarman, the actors' agent, planted himself at my table.

The stories sometimes seem intended for people who already know Hollywood and environs. You almost feel that Turner is telling them to a crony, late at night, at a table at the Derby or Musso-Frank's, and you're simply overhearing them. The reader, as is true with many an eavesdropper, doesn't always get all the details. But the best parts—the puzzle, the violence, the dames—get across.

Women were one of Dan Turner's specialties and he excelled at describing them and his activities with them:

> It was a dame who barged into me. She was an auburn-haired, curvesome cutie with violet eyes, bee-stung lips and a figure like seven million bucks. She was dressed in a tweed sports outfit that was tailored to her shapely form like melted wax.

> I recognized the wren. She was Janet Moore, the Bonham kid's co-star in that new Titanic pic; a taffy-haired muffin whose gorgeous exterior concealed a heart as big as a birdseed.

> Copious quantities of Yolande's alluring epidermis were on display, but none of it as white as her frightened pan. To put it in a capsule, she was a double-barreled knockout in a triple distilled funk.

* * *

A brunette jane was lying there, half out of the mussed covers. She might have been pretty, once. Her body was still attractive enough. A tissue-sheer nightgown gave intimate hints at the swelling hills of her soft white breasts and the creamy smoothness of her shoulders and arms. But her pan wasn't nice to look at. It was contorted, colorless; stark fear was frozen in her glassy eyes. There was a scorched hole in the pillow alongside her. And the top of her skull was blown open.

She was as dead as vaudeville.

I lifted my head, took a gander at the she-male charms that were almost fully displayed by that strapless gown. I ran a finger over her white shoulders, and tingles started skittering through my veins. Her skin was smoother than satin, whiter than milk. I did a job on it with my lips, concentrating on the soft throbbing hollow of her neck.

She gasped and pressed herself even closer to me. I jammed her back against the wall, mashed her breast with the pressure of my chest. "Baby," I whispered, "this is one scene that isn't going to be play-acting—"

From the doorway, a roscoe said: "*Ka-chow!*" and a slug creased the side of my noggin. Neon lights exploded inside my think-tank.

Even outside the boudoir Turner led an active, hazardous life. He both dished it out and took it:

He said: "You son of a ——!" and started to blam the barrel of his rod down on my dome. That's what I'd been hoping for. I swerved, ducked—and catapulted full-tilt at the window. I took the whole damned sash with me, glass and all. I went sailing out into the night before he could get his roscoe lined into firing position.

A sleepy chink maid in pajamas answered my ring. She was a cute little slant-eyed number. I said, "Is Mr. Pulznak home?" She shook her head. "Him on location in Fresno. Been gone two weeks." I said, "Thanks, I'll have a gander for myself." I pushed past her. She started to yip . . . "Shut up!" I growled. She kept on trying to make noise. So I popped her on the button. She dropped.

An ugly hunch bit me on the brisket. I growled: "Hey, what the hell are *you* doing here? What's cooking?" and made a lunge at her.
But she was too sudden for me. She flipped across the room toward the open front door; picked up a brass book-end en route. She slammed the gadget at me; pitched a perfect strike. It took me full in the features, bounced off my button and rendered me unconscious.

I didn't get a hinge at him. He gave me no chance to defend myself. He tiptoed up behind me and flailed me on the noggin with a blunt instrument, whereupon I went bye-bye.

A private dick needs a thick conk if he hopes to stay in business, and mine has taken many a flogging without getting shattered. I opened my bleary glims and mumbled mushily: "Durable Dan Turner, that's me. Knock him down and win a cigar."

Surprisingly the innumerable bops on the coco didn't addle Turner's wits. He managed, almost always, to play fair with the reader and end each chronicle with a summing up of how he arrived at his solution. To his pal Dave Donaldson of Homicide he'd say:

> Well, there it is. I knew it had to be Del Cavallero when I found out that Myrrla Montaine was well fixed for dough. She couldn't have had any reason for blackmailing Waldermann. Del Cavallero was the only other person who had any hold on Sid. Therefore, Del Cavallero wasn't really dead; he was behind the Montaine murder-mess. And I figured he'd come out in the open after Sid saw him on the stairway to Connie Bowen's apartment stash. He wanted to threaten Sid into keeping quiet. He biffed Connie so she wouldn't hear the conversation; that's why she's out cold in the hallway.

Spicy Detective's publishers branched out in 1937, adding a slightly more sedate title to their list. *Private Detective Stories* sold for fifteen cents, probably because its stories and pictures weren't as spicy as those of its twenty-five-cent sister. A Dan Turner story, "Murder on the Sound

Stage," led off the first issue, which promised on its cover "Intimate Revelations of Private Investigators." *Spicy Detective* itself held on until late in 1942, having produced 104 steamy issues, and then changed its name to the less provocative *Speed Detective*. Dan Turner appeared there, too.

Also in 1942 came *Dan Turner, Hollywood Detective*, a pulp devoted entirely to the exploits of the movie colony snoop. Whereas hero pulps offered one novel about Doc Savage or the Shadow per issue, this magazine provided a mix of at least a half dozen novelets and short stories starring nobody else but Dan Turner. As a bonus there was usually an eight-page Dan Turner adventure in black-and-white comic book format, written by Bellem and drawn by Adolphe Barreaux. By its second year the pulp's title was modified to just plain *Hollywood Detective*, but Turner continued to dominate most of the issues. According to Robert Sampson in *Mystery, Detective and Espionage Magazines*, a good portion of the yarns were reprints, although "nowhere in the magazine was there a hint that the contents had been published before."

Dan Turner managed to get some attention outside the pulpwood field, too. S. J. Perelman, a studious reader of the pulps, did a piece on him for *The New Yorker* in the 1940s. Entitled "Somewhere a Roscoe . . . ," it was a typical Perelman blend of scornful parody and grudging affection. He was plainly fascinated by Dan Turner, calling him "the apotheosis of all private eyes. Out of Ma Barker by Dashiell Hammett's Sam Spade."

The Tinseltown gumshoe's career came to an end in the late summer of 1950 with the final issue of *Hollywood Detective*. The last number was digest size. "Inside, you found seven stories," says Sampson. "Three of these were about Dan Turner and were signed by Bellem. The others, signed by other names, some patently fake, appeared to be by Bellem also." Bellem went on to become a fairly successful television writer, turning out scripts for shows like *The Lone Ranger, Dick Tracy, Boston Blackie, 77 Sunset Strip, Tarzan,* and *Superman.* He died in Sherman Oaks, California, in 1968.

The folks responsible for bringing Dan Turner and his colleagues before the public did business under a number of corporate names, the most frequently used being Culture Publications and the Trojan Publishing Corporation. It seems likely that this latter name was a homage to the well-known contraceptive and just as likely that Dan Turner always drank Vat 69 chiefly because of the sexual connotation of the number. Under various designations, the publishing companies were incorporated in a number of states and published hither and yon. But all editorial offices were to be found in the vicinity of 480 Lexington Avenue in Manhattan. This was also where DC Comics was headquartered from the late 1930s onward and where *Action Comics, Detective Comics,* and other funny books featuring Superman, Batman, Sandman, the Spectre, Dr. Fate, Green Arrow, and others originated.

The link between the comics and the pulps was an aggressive and enterprising fellow named Harry Donenfeld. Publisher, printer, distributor, Donenfeld was a silent partner in Culture and Trojan. The professed publisher was Frank Armer, who actually put his name on many of the pulps. In tandem or in combination with others, Armer and Donenfeld were responsible for such

1930s publications as *Love Revels*, *Gay Parisienne*, *Stocking Parade*, *Bedtime Stories*, *Silk Stocking Stories*, *Stolen Sweets*, *Snappy Detective Stories*, and the Spicy and Speed lines. Donenfeld had taken over the comic books from the pioneering but underfunded Major Malcolm Wheeler-Nicholson and was thus able to benefit from the enormous profits that Superman and his kin brought in. Although Donenfeld tried to keep the relatively wholesome comics and the raunchy pulps separate in the public mind, *Writer's Digest* often listed DC Comics as Trojan Publications and gave the same address for both operations.

Spicy Detective housed a great many other detectives, although none was quite as colorful as Dan Turner. There was a similar mix to that found in the somewhat more respectable mystery pulps—private eyes, reporters, and cops. One of the brighter lights of the magazine was Tim Sloan, an eye who also appeared in *Private Detective* and whose capers were signed by a variety of pen names, including Dale Boyd and Wallace Kayton. The stories were told with some humor and Sloan was not exactly your usual tough detective:

> The door opened and Tim Sloan came in. Tim Sloan was six foot six and skinny. Not thin, skinny. She knew where Tim had been last night, knew what banquets always did to him. His face was lugubrious, his long, thin nose red and quivering, his mouth an inverted vee. Hair poured out of his hat and over his left eye. The top button of his shirt was missing and the tie was twisted askew. He was dragging—not carrying—a topcoat.

And he walked with the solemn, conscious dignity of a man who is drunk and tries to convince himself he does not show it.

His secretary was a bit out of the ordinary, too:

She was short, and plump and dumpy in flatheeled, sensible shoes. Her hair was mousy, nondescript; her eyes vague blue behind thick spectacles. Her nose was fat and shiny—but so was the rest of her face. She had a law degree, a savings account, a cell at the Y.W.C.A. and two manias. One was underthings. She liked to imagine the sensual slither of pastel silk about her sturdy hips and thighs; an exciting cradle of provocative lace on her full breasts. Tim Sloan was her other mania.

Yet in the four years that she had worked for him, woman's man though he was, Tim Sloan had never caressed Emma Hohenberger. Neither had she ever worn silk underwear.

His cases in both magazines were similar P.I. fare, but *Private Detective* had less creamy flesh and frilly lingerie.

There was also Joe Trimo, adventures credited to one Horton Jacques, a tough—and horny—P.I. who was most often involved in cases of political chicanery. Joe had a colorful style, especially when it came to describing women:

She was a pretty cute waitress. The skirt of her uniform barely covered her knees, and from there down to her ankles her legs were silk-hosed and shapely. She had a mop of black hair and a front elevation that looked like she'd taken a deep breath and never quit holding it.

Among the others included on the *Spicy* roster were Bill Carter, Jarnegan, Mike Cockrell, and S. W. Humphrey— whose initials allegedly stood for Smith & Wesson. E. Hoffmann Price, usually not bothering to hide behind an alias, cooked up several series dicks for the pulp—Honest John Carmody, Jeff Dargan, and Cliff Cargin. These last two both started as New Orleans ops and eventually settled in San Francisco.

Contrary to what might be expected, quite a few of the stories in *Spicy Detective* had coherent plots, fairly believable, though oversexed characters, and convincing settings. By blue-penciling the references to flimsy underwear and milk-white flesh, the majority of the stories could have run in any of the middle-range detective pulps. Actually the reverse is probably what often happened. After a story was bounced by other, better-paying markets (*Spicy Detective* paid from half a cent to one cent per word), the addition of a few paragraphs of sexy stuff might result in a sale. As Will Murray points out in his study of the Spicy pulps in *Risque Stories*, the pulp "was a wide open market with a reputation for paying quickly." Norman Daniels, Hugh B. Cave, and Wyatt Blassingame were other frequent contributors.

In addition to its prose, *Spicy Detective* was distinguished from its statelier rivals by its artwork. The covers, usually by H. J. Ward, always showcased a young woman who was not exactly naked. He "painted his girls in attractive, girl-next-door strokes," says Murray, "and gave them enough clothes to preserve their decency without minimizing their charms. . . . Regardless of the pose or situation—and some were pretty wild—the Spicy Girl always looked wholesome, virginal, yet tantalizing." The magazine consistently provided many more interior illustrations than any other detective pulp. An average issue of *Black Mask*, for example, had at best a half dozen or so. *Spicy*, on the other hand, always offered over two dozen. And each and every drawing featured at least one young woman in her undies or less.

One of the most frequently seen illustrators was Adolphe Barreaux. He once told me, "I first met Frank Armer socially in 1925. In 1928, when I abandoned show business to set up my studio as an illustrator, I immediately began to do some work for Frank." Barreaux's art, therefore, graced *Spicy Detective* from the very first issue. He designed the montage of put-upon and scantily clad girls that framed the contents page and, later, drew the tiny spot—two cops, a dead woman in her underwear—that decorated the magazine's spine.

Other regulars were H. V. Parkhurst, Rex Maxon, and Max Plaisted. Parkhurst, a veteran illustrator who also painted an occasional cover, went on to draw *Hopalong Cassidy* comic books in the forties. Maxon, moonlighting from his regular job of drawing the daily *Tarzan* newspaper strip, never signed his work. Plaisted made up in determination what he lacked in technical skill and was the most frequent illuminator of the Dan Turner saga. In fact, he was the definitive depicter, as identified with the Hollywood snoop as John Tenniel is with Alice.

The Armer-Donenfeld combine had a hand in several

other pulps in the thirties. *Snappy Detective* and *Candid Detective* did not thrive. *Romantic Detective* held on for a year or so late in the decade. A fifteen-cent bimonthly that fell somewhere between *Spicy Detective* and *Private Detective*, it had nothing much to do with love. Bellem, Blassingame, and Roger Torrey contributed, sometimes under their own names. *Super-Detective*, having hit the stands briefly in the early 1930s, returned again in 1940 and managed to last for over ten years.

Chapter 8

Dangerous Dames

Usually, women detectives are not favorites with men readers.

—*The Editor,*
Crime Busters,
December 1938

There were plenty of women to be found in the detective pulps, especially on the covers. Mainly, however, they appeared as victims and then in such occupations as gun moll, floozie, sweetheart, and gray-haired mother. Since most of the readers of this genre were male, the notion of a female detective starring in her own series was not felt by most editors and publishers to have much appeal, especially back then when even the concept of equal rights for women hadn't caught on with a majority of the population. Occasionally a magazine would go against the trend and make room for a lady eye. And so in the 1930s and 1940s several practiced their trade in the pages of the pulpwoods, including one or two notable ones. All the stories, by the way, were written by men.

While the male of the species had begun to proliferate, though not too rapidly, in the 1920s, no hard-boiled lady private eyes showed up to compete in that decade. Typical of what was to be found instead are Hulbert Footner's novelets and serials about Madame Storey. These appeared in *Argosy* from 1922 through 1935. Madame Storey is beautiful and ladylike. "Her clothing is high fashion. Her offices and rooms are planned settings," says Robert Sampson in *Yesterday's Faces*. "She casts an atmosphere of dramatic tension. Around her glows the essence of the French salon, carefully nurtured. It's indispensable to the conduct of her business. As are the cigarette and the monkey." The lady detective is a chain-smoker and keeps a pet monkey. The stories have Madame Storey moving through all levels of society, yet basically they strive to achieve the sort of slick-paper feel to be found in the work of Oppenheim and his many competitors.

Nor was a single hard-boiled lady eye to be found in hardcover mystery novels in the 1920s, a situation that remained pretty much the same throughout the 1930s. The audience that patronized the public and rental libraries was considerably more sedate, and while it did support a number of female sleuths—mostly the meddlesome spinster or the bright, fashionable young amateur—there was apparently little demand for the rougher approaches to detection. It wasn't until 1939 and the publication of Erle Stanley Gardner's *The Bigger They Come* that hardcover readers got a tough female op of their own. Written under the pen name of A. A. Fair, the novel introduced big, gruff Bertha Cool and her junior partner, Donald Lam. By then several tough female detectives had already set up shop in the pulps. The first important one was the creation of Cleve F. Adams, and quite probably veteran pulp writer Gardner had read her adventures and kept them in mind.

Adams makes critics and historians of mystery fiction uneasy. In the early 1940s, when his hardcover novels were being published, Anthony Boucher admitted to feelings of

A representative cover from the heyday of *Black Mask* (January, 1937).

The Maltese Falcon

By DASHIELL HAMMETT

A *Maltese Falcon* illustration from the November, 1929, issue of *Black Mask*.

Race Williams shooting
'em up in the pages
of *Dime Detective*
(November, 1939).

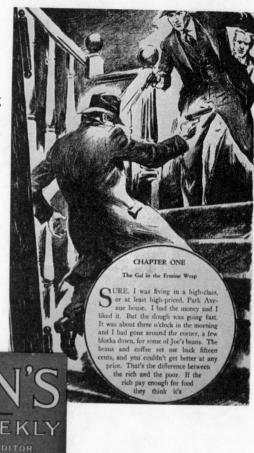

CHAPTER ONE

The Gal in the Ermine Wrap

SURE, I was living in a high-class,
or at least high-priced, Park Avenue house. I had the money and I
liked it. But the dough was going fast.
It was about three o'clock in the morning
and I had gone around the corner, a few
blocks down, for some of Joe's beans. The
beans and coffee set me back fifteen
cents, and you couldn't get better at any
price. That's the difference between
the rich and the poor. If the
rich pay enough for food
they think it's

The author himself
posing as his detective
(December 13, 1924).

THE DUCHESS
OF DIAMONDS

A Rambler Novelette

by Fred MacIsaac

Author of "Fall-Guy," etc.

That roving red-headed newshound had been dodging women all his life. Marriage was the one thing he was afraid of—but when a gang of smart jewel thieves snatched the current blonde on his trail he couldn't let well enough alone. He had to get her back—along with an atrocity in gold-and-diamonds—only to have her tell him she wouldn't marry under any circumstances.

The man in evening dress clubbed the revolver down on Murphy's head.

Rambler Murphy about to get slugged. Art by *Dime Detective*'s resident illustrator, John Fleming Gould (February, 1938).

MANDARIN'S
JADE

Which introduces John Dalmas, investigator extraordinary, and fifty-one bits of priceless carved jade that kept a parade of cock-eyed characters, headed by a dizzy drunken blonde, dodging bullets through twenty-four mad murder hours.

That's Dalmas, forerunner of Philip Marlowe, getting roughed up on the floor (*Dime Detective*, November, 1937).

The dark woman slapped the chloroform-soaked handkerchief against my face.

by Raymond Chandler

Sally in action in an early issue of *Spicy Detective*
(May, 1938), encountering a villain with
a sense of humor.

I knew what was coming, but I couldn't break loose from her in time to duck.

"Outside, sweetheart," I said softly, "we're going for a little ride."

CLYDA CARLO

She jammed the end of a roscoe at me. "Just a minute," she said. "I want to talk to you."

I whirled, and my gun was in my hand. I don't like people who come up behind me like that.

Some typical events in the life of Dan Turner, Hollywood detective. Art by the incomparable Max Plaisted.

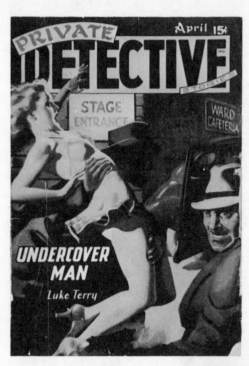

Showing the decorative side of private investigation (April, 1942).

Yet another decorative cover (January, 1943).

A cover by Rafael DeSoto
illustrating the wartime
yarn "This Is the Way
We Bake Our Dead"
(June, 1943).

Another handsome
DeSoto effort
(March, 1941).

Nicely designed,
and informative
(July 13, 1935).

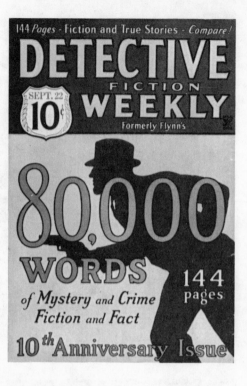

Daffy Dill going after
the news in *Detective
Fiction Weekly*
(September 28, 1935).

Showcasing an
Erle Stanley Gardner yarn
it was difficult to ask for
by name (May, 1941).

Red Goose

*The picture was framed—and so
was everyone in the deal*

One of Davis's earliest
appearances in *Black
Mask* (February, 1934).

By NORBERT DAVIS

DEATH ON DUTY

By ROGER TORREY
Author of "Don't Stake Out the Morgue," etc.

You want to heist a cash register, you take your rod, sure, and you eliminate any coppers that get in your way—What you want to watch, though, is eliminating too many coppers!

He had his gun half out of the holster when the lug cracked Sellers with the blackjack, and then he heard: "Hold it, copper! Hold tight!"

Jack Kirby's illustration for a Torrey story in the April, 1941, issue of *Detective Short Stories*.

A portrait of one of Erle Stanley Gardner's masked marvels (September 22, 1934).

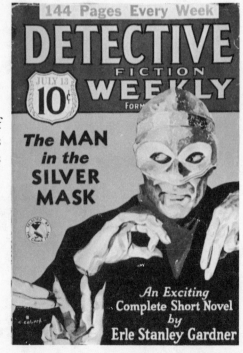

Cardigan getting into trouble in the bowels of Chinatown. Painting by Walter Baumhofer (April, 1936), who was also the *Doc Savage* cover artist.

The contents page of the very first issue, offering a little something for everybody.

SPICY DETECTIVE STORIES is published by the CULTURE PUBLICATIONS, INC., 900 Market Street, Wilmington, Delaware.

Another wartime DeSoto cover (September, 1942).

You'll have to read the magazine to find out why they aren't named Tom, Dick, and Harry (March, 1948).

Lamont Cranston's nemesis, the Oriental master villain Shiwan Khan, appears to have some tricks up his ornate sleeves in a 1939 issue of *The Shadow*.

The Green Lama in
a mystical pose,
from the pages of
Double Detective
(August, 1940).

The
Green
Lama

A nicely designed cover
by Rudolph Belarski
(July, 1938), who went on to
paint numerous paperback
covers in the 1940s.

Carrie Cashin, fully clothed for a change,
from the pages of *Crime Busters* (February, 1938).

Violet McDade in the midst of bullets and bloodshed,
as usual (November, 1937).

ambivalence while reviewing *Up Jumped the Devil*. He found it "a grand piece of ultra-hardboiled action and dialogue in the toughest tradition, and at the same time a very nasty piece of work." Boucher went on to point out that "the author has utter comtempt for anyone who is not a white Nordic." And he quotes what was to become the most often quoted line Adams ever penned. When private dick Rex McBride is accused of using Gestapo methods, he replies, "An American gestapo is goddam well what we need!" In a 1975 essay in *The Armchair Detective* Francis M. Nevins commends Adams for his "incomparable raw readability." But he also points out that the typical Adams detective—be he using the name McBride, Bill Rye, John J. Shannon, or Steve McCloud—"is a supreme male chauvinist" as well as "a fascist, a racist, a cynic and a hypocrite." *Private Eyes: 101 Knights*, by Robert A. Baker and Michael T. Nietzel, came out in 1985. The authors argue that Adams's private eyes "are unique personalities who add new dimensions to the genre." They then admit that the typical hero is crude and uneducated and that he possesses "a cynical, fascist heart."

Cleve Franklin Adams was about forty when he began selling to the pulps. He had been, by his own account, a copper miner, a detective, a movie art director, an interior decorator, and a life insurance executive. He once confessed, "I finally decided that the only way I could capitalize on a life-time's mistakes was to write about them." He was fairly successful from the mid-1930s on, selling stories, novelets, and serials to such magazines as *Detective Fiction Weekly*, *Argosy*, *Dime Detective*, *Black Mask*, and *Double Detective*. He turned out, for the most part, readable hard-boiled work. Writing for book publication, away from the restraints of the newsstand, seems to have brought out the worst in him. There's no denying that his fascism, sexism, and racism came out of the closet in many of his P.I. novels of the forties. Considering this, it's interesting that Adams's first major pulp series was about a pair of lady private eyes, one of whom was Mexican.

The stories, starring Violet McDade and narrated by her partner, Nevada Alvarado, began appearing in Street & Smith's *Clues* in 1935. Although the detective agency was called McDade & Alvarado, Violet was clearly the boss of the setup. She was surely one of the most formidable private eyes to practice in Hollywood and environs and just about the only one who'd formerly been a circus fat lady. Her weight fluctuated between three hundred and four hundred pounds, depending on whether or not she'd been dieting. Like many of her male contemporaries, including all of those later cooked up by Adams, Violet had a rough, tough exterior shielding a sentimental core. Capable of scooping up any loose cash she might find lying around the scene of a crime, she would also tear up a client's check if she decided he wasn't on the level.

Nevada was slim, dark-haired, and pretty. Not quite as clever or cunning as Violet, she was fairly hard-boiled:

> I caught the woman's wrist, flipped up my gun and jammed it into her side—hard. "Open your hand," I said. "Open it—or I'll put a slug right through your girdle!"

She shared most Hollywood P.I.s' awareness of the phoniness behind the glitter:

It was attractive at night; ugly as sin in broad
daylight. A great big barn of a place, it was
frequented by the fast set, which included anybody that had money enough to stand the tariff.
You could find Hollywood's highest-paid stars
there on occasion. You could also find the stumble
bum who had made a lucky buy at Santa Anita
that afternoon. In between were the usual tour-
ists from Iowa, ga-ga at the tinsel splendor, eager
to pay ten bucks a fifth for dollar California
champagne.

Her feelings about her enormous partner were, to say
the least, mixed, as indicated in these openings from two of
the novelets:

Violet McDade was throwing a party. And, like
most of Violet's parties, this one boded ill for my
peace of mind. We were due to dock at San Pedro
in the morning. This was the last night of the
cruise—the night traditionally set aside for the
captain's ball—the night of all nights that Violet
would pick to embarrass me.
There were times when she infuriated me so
that I could quite cheerfully have emptied my
little .32 into her fat middle. But I never did.
Cold logic always came to my rescue. As her
partner I was making more money than any dick,
male or female, would risk losing. Besides, I liked
the creature. There was a third reason, one that
perhaps bore more weight than the other two

combined: She was faster than a rattlesnake with those two sleeve guns of hers.

Her moonface a mask of smug complacency, Violet McDade was lolling at her desk when the girl was announced. There was never any happy medium about Violet; she was either utterly and sloppily relaxed, or a mountainous female whirlwind; a two-fisted enlargement of Tugboat Annie, if you get the picture. Five years as the lesser half of McDade & Alvarado should have accustomed me to her peculiarities, but somehow her apparent lack of interest in a new client always infuriated me to the point of distraction.

I remarked as much, and added bitingly, "You might at least wipe some of the mustard off your mouth!" It was only three in the afternoon, but Violet had been eating again. I mean, she'd had lunch at one, and then, at two thirty, had sent out for what she referred to as "just a snack." The remnants of the snack still cluttered her desk.

She opened her little greenish eyes and regarded me with sleepy appraisal. "You know, Nevada, they's times you make me sick. Sicker'n usual, I mean. First place, your reference to the mustard on my mouth is a—now—rank calumny, on account of you know I don't like mustard. And in the second place, we already got more business than we need, so what the hell? If this dame is so snooty she don't like my looks, she can get herself another dick." Her fat, beringed hands did, however, make an abortive attempt to straighten her desk.

Violet practiced a sort of kidding racism with Nevada, addressing her now and then as "Mex." On the occasion when a cousin of Nevada's got the best of one of their operatives, Violet criticized the guy with "Just the same, Clancy, you're a disgrace to the Irish, lettin' a Mex beat—" Stamping her foot, Nevada says, "You—you lout! My family dates back beyond the conquistadors and the Spanish grants. Where did you come from? A circus tent! One more slurring remark out of you and I'll—"

Despite her bulk, Violet was certainly no armchair detective. She was hyperactive when pursuing a killer or one of the many insurance cheats the agency specialized in nabbing. She hopped in and out of cabs and cars, ran pell-mell down alleys, paused to do a little dancing on a nightclub floor. Her twin guns were usually fatal to hoodlums, and even when she simply slapped someone, it was quite effective: "Violet hit him. Not hard, just a backhanded sweep of the arm that hurled him across the room."

The most successful lady eye of the pulps was undoubtedly Carrie Cashin, who made her debut in the first issue of Street & Smith's *Crime Busters* (November 1937). Theodore Tinsley was the author and her initial case led off the magazine. The photo cover showed a pretty chestnut-haired model portraying Carrie as she climbed out a window, her thigh holster plainly in view. Although a clever, intuitive young woman, Carrie favored a system of detection that put much of the emphasis on physical fitness. In nearly all of her cases acrobatics is more important than ratiocination. She appeared, between 1937 and 1942, in over three dozen breathless, impatient narratives in which nothing was allowed to stand in the way of headlong movement. Possessed of a highly personal sense of justice, Carrie had little respect for rules. In the course of her active career she violated quite a few existing laws. Breaking and entering was one of her favorite devices and she was not above armed robbery or even a little polite kidnaping.

Headquartered in Manhattan, Carrie was the senior partner in the Cash And Carry Detective Agency. The name of the agency, as Tinsley never tired of pointing out, "was an amusing reversal of Carrie Cashin's own name." Her partner, sometimes referred to as "her stooge," was a tough, amiable fellow named Aleck Burton. Not quite as bright or as foolhardy as Carrie, Aleck fronted for her by pretending to be the boss of the outfit. "That was because most clients had a silly prejudice against women detectives. So broad-shouldered Aleck usually posed as the head of the agency and accepted the cases. But it was Carrie who delivered the goods!" Tinsley once said, "It was a historical novelty to have a smart woman and a very dumb male working together." A former department store detective, Carrie's standard fee was $1,000.

When we first meet her, in a story entitled "White Elephant," she is in the process of committing a burglary. Climbing out of a hotel room window in broad daylight and making her way along a stone balcony, Carrie retrieves an allegedly stolen curio—a small statue of an elephant—from the adjoining room of the suspected thief. When she returns to her room, she finds that the body of her client— "stabbed in the throat, savagely enough to sever an artery"—is now on the floor beside the bed. Then the hotel dick starts pounding on the door.

The pace continues like this. Indeed, Tinsley constructed all of Carrie's subsequent cases—"Blue Murder," "Black Queen," "Riddle in Silk," "The Man with Green Whiskers," "Miami Murder," etc.—in a similar headlong way. These novelets are really miniature novels, in the Doc Savage, Phantom Detective, Avenger tradition—rich with action and violence, strange crimes and stranger villains. And quite probably it was only Carrie's gender that kept her from graduating into a whole pulpwood devoted to her. "The single most popular and promising character to appear in *Crime Busters*," Will Murray has said in an article on the magazine, "was Theodore Tinsley's Carrie Cashin. She might have had a chance in a magazine of her own, but Street & Smith never went ahead with the idea." Editor John Nanovic made it a point to find out exactly what his readers felt about the magazine. The first issue and subsequent ones contained a ballot to pick the three favorite stories. Those responding would get a free copy of one of S&S's lesser pulps. Carrie consistently did very well in these polls, her stories always finishing among the top three. In his editorial in the December 1938 issue Nanovic referred to her as "probably the most popular woman detective in fiction today," as well as the only one who'd overcome the male mystery fans' aversion to lady sleuths.

Recalling the series many years later, Tinsley stated that for him it had been a "change of pace." At the time he was also ghosting several Shadow novels a year. He felt his detective owed something to the Spicy line of pulpwoods— "Villains were always trying to tear her clothes off, and the like." The prose in Carrie's stories was considerably tamer than that to be found in a magazine like *Spicy Detective*, and Earl Mayan's illustrations were much more sophisticated (he was already looking ahead to the sort of thing he'd later do in *The Saturday Evening Post*) than those to be found decorating the capers of Dan Turner. Tinsley, of course, never let his readers forget that they were dealing with a female sleuth:

> Carrie was dressed in a shimmering evening gown that emphasized the softly rounded beauty of her figure. Aleck gulped as he stared at her.

> Carrie, watching from the inside of the tent, could feel the thrill of the crowd. But she knew she had no time to delay, if she was to carry out the daring plan she had already formulated. She whirled away from the peephole and began swiftly to wriggle out of her clothing.
> To disrobe was only the work of a few seconds. Carrie's dress had a zipper that released the garment with almost a single jerk. Shoes and slippers followed. Carrie Cashin stood barefooted, dressed in an exact replica of the diver's silken swim suit.

Carrie wasn't the only one who disrobed in the stories:

> "You heard me, wise baby! You're goin' down in that cellar opening. I ain't takin' no chances on you runnin' out on me for awhile. Peel—or I'll do it for you!"
> With her face aflame, Annette lifted her slip over her cringing shoulders. She held it bunched for an instant at the back of her head. She was hoping she might make a sudden clutch for the

man's gun. Annette realized she was an alluring figure in her cute, shell-pink brassiere and panties. But her lure didn't work. The hackman's glance remained grimly alert for treachery.

Violence was also plentiful in the cases of Carrie Cashin:

Then, from the rear of the filing cabinet's drawer, a shining automatic jerked. It whirled circlewise in the clenched hand of Carrie Cashin. It jammed into the ribs of the surprised Mr. Hanley with a force that made him grunt.

"Drop that rod, boy friend!"

He took one surprised look at the girl and her steady gun. His own weapon clattered to the floor. As his hands raised above his head, Aleck darted forward. A double click sounded, and Hanley was helplessly fettered. But as Aleck stepped closer to him, the captive suddenly smashed down with his cuffed hands in a vicious swing at Aleck's skull.

The blow never landed. Carrie's gun butt hit Hanley in back of the ear, tumbling him into a dazed heap on the floor.

Snarling, he clutched at Carrie's leg as she tried to sway to her feet. He tumbled her headlong. His hand twisted in her hair and pulled her head fiercely back. Finally he fumbled at her taut throat.

Carrie's teeth broke the hold. But she knew she was no match for her opponent's brute strength.

. . . Her eyes closed tightly. Breathless, half fainting, she managed to shove the pinioned arm farther back. Farther.

Craaack!

Casaba's arm had snapped between wrist and elbow. He went down on his face, groveling for his fallen gun. Carrie beat him to it.

Crime Busters changed its name to *Mystery Magazine* with the November 1939 issue. Carrie carried on her career there until nearly the end. Her final bow was in "The Unusual Mr. Smith" (November 1942). Once, during a restless and bored spell, she complained, "If I was Sherlock Holmes, I could at least play the violin—or smoke a smelly black pipe—or jab myself in the arm with a needle. That's the trouble with being a female detective. You always have to remember that you're a lady!"

Detective Fiction Weekly's Sarah Watson was neither glamorous nor petite. Of middle years and heavyset, the owner of the Watson Detective Agency dressed in square-toed shoes and rusty black skirts and shirtwaists. She was tough enough to threaten a reluctant informant with "For fifty thousand, I'd even beat a man up. I'd like to beat up a man proper, for once. I'd begin on the nose, Jessup. The nose is a nice, tender place to begin. Maybe I'd break it—after a while. Talk, Mr. Jessup. Talk!" Yet she usually lunched off buns she carried in a soiled paper bag, and she addressed her assistant, a lean red-haired young man, as "whippersnapper." Sort of small-town hard-boiled is what the stories, written by D. B. McCandless, were. They began late in 1936 and appeared several times during the next year.

A sex object first and a detective second, Sally the Sleuth graced the pages of *Spicy Detective* from 1934 onward. Her cases were chronicled in comic book style and given two black-and-white pages in every issue. A true pioneer, Sally was doing her pulp detection before most of the other ladies we've discussed thus far. She also managed to appear in comic book format long before such male heroes as Superman and Batman, who didn't get started until 1938 and 1939 respectively. Sally was not exactly a private eye, but a sort of plainclothes cop who worked for the Chief, a handsome fellow in a snap-brim hat. Her plain clothes didn't stay on her long, since Sally lost most of her outer garments in just about every investigation. Villains never ran out of plausible-sounding reasons for ordering her to "take off those clothes—Or I'll tear them off!" Her standard working outfit, therefore, was usually bra and panties. One spy case ends with her holding up her underwear to an FBI agent who's asked the whereabouts of the missing formula. Sally explains, "You'll find it written in invisible ink on the trimming of my panties." She also got tied up a lot.

Sally the Sleuth was created and drawn by Adolphe Barreaux, who always signed his own name to the strip. Barreaux, who had a simple, effective cartoon style, operated an art service in the 1930s, and the Spicy line was one of his chief clients. He also found time to contribute work, of a somewhat less sexy nature, to the first original-material comic book, Major Malcolm Wheeler-Nicholson's *New Fun Comics*. Sally outlived *Spicy* and continued to catch crooks, although shedding fewer garments, in its successor, *Speed Detective*.

In the forties, after the departure of Carrie Cashin,

female P.I.'s virtually vanished. All the other lady ops who'd arrived in the thirties were long gone by the time World War II got going, and few new ones were added. This particular branch of the profession never did flourish again in the few years the pulps had remaining.

Chapter 9

Gentlemen of the Press

Newspaper reporters shared many of the characteristics of the private eye. They were tough, cynical, and dogged in their pursuit of the truth—or at least a close enough approximation of the truth to serve their purposes. Many of them dressed in similar fashion to the hard-boiled dicks, favoring well-worn trench coats or overcoats and disreputable hats worn at jaunty angles. They also had a fondness for the cheap booze served in speakeasies and saloons. Not surprisingly, then, quite a few of them showed up in the pulps, especially in the 1930s, doubling as detectives. *Black Mask*, for example, featured four major newshawk sleuths and several lesser ones during the decade.

By the early thirties the fast-talking, two-fisted reporter was already a staple of popular entertainment. One of the chief reasons for this was Ben Hecht and Charles MacArthur's *The Front Page*. The play, a hard-boiled comedy about crime and corruption, opened on Broadway in August 1928 and was an impressive hit. The long lean Lee Tracy starred as Hildy Johnson, a "bustling and fast-talking newspaperman." Tracy was to play variations of this role for the next several years, blending a wisecracking cynicism with a sort of shopworn integrity and managing to convey the impression that he was both unfailingly astute and moderately sozzled. Both the actor and the play were highly influential on the mass entertainments of the thirties. "The smart-mouth, cynical reporters gathered in the pressroom of the Chicago Criminal Courts Building," Richard Schickel has pointed out, "served as the model for generations of fictional journalists. In the 1930s, a lively Hollywood genre in which similarly endowed newsmen solved crimes and served justice under high deadline pressure—yelling, slamming in and out of doors, ripping out their front pages—while never missing a gag line, was obviously inspired by the Hecht-MacArthur success."

In 1931 *The Front Page* came to the screen, with Pat O'Brien as Hildy Johnson. O'Brien became one of the masters of this sort of part, going on to portray tough wise-guy newsmen in several other films. Hollywood also got hold of Lee Tracy, casting him as a brash reporter in *Born Reckless* (1930), *Doctor X* (1932), *Blessed Event* (1932), and *Advice to the Lovelorn* (1933), an extremely loose adaptation of Nathanael West's novel *Miss Lonelyhearts*. The columnists in some of these movies were based on Walter Winchell, then a very successful and influential purveyor of Broadway gossip. Winchell also served as the role model for at least one of the pulpwood newshounds.

The newsroom melodrama was often similar to the gangster films of the era. "They have the same brash energy," says Nick Roddick in *A New Deal in Entertainment*, "the same fast-talking characters, often operating on the fringes of the underworld, and the same linchpin of determined action within a socially specific context."

The earliest of the new breed of reporter-detective was not actually a star but a costar. Kennedy, of the *Richmond City Free Press*, was introduced in the September 1928 issue of *Black Mask*. He shared the story, and the subsequent series, with police captain Steve MacBride. Frederick Nebel wrote just over three dozen stories about these characters, all of them filled with thorough police work and fast, wild action. MacBride was a tough, honest cop with a streetwise sense of humor. Kennedy was something else again, a considerably more complex character.

"Kennedy, when first introduced, is neatly dressed, sober and not particularly fragile," says Dave Lewis in his essay on Nebel, "The Backbone of Black Mask." That soon changes and Kennedy becomes a drunk, sometimes exhibiting the alcoholic's short temper and nastiness. He is also, however, a man with a stubborn, almost obsessive belief in seeing justice done. Threats of legal action, physical violence, or even death can't dissuade him. He fights very hard to remain hopeful.

His creator clearly admires Kennedy, yet he is concerned about his way of life and is sometimes perplexed by his self-destructive behavior. He describes him this way in "Bad News," a wintry tale in which the reporter plays the lead: "He shivered to his marrow. His threadbare coat was really a spring coat. He never wore gloves. His socks were silk and his shoes were thin. Rubbers he never used. He looked like a scarecrow or like the shadow of an emaciated tree." Near the end of this story, after Kennedy realizes that the girl he's been trying to help really isn't worth it, Nebel says: "Kennedy let go her hand. He looked very dejected. He leaned back against the door, his mouth sagging, his face very gray and worn by years of drinking, late hours, little sleep. The world seemed to him a very cockeyed place, full of more wrongs than rights."

Kennedy is also a wise guy. He tends to be irreverent when everyone else is being pious, brashly truthful when all others are hypocritical. This prompts people to advise him to "Cut out horsing," and sometimes to take a poke at him. Although MacBride has a great deal of respect for the newsman's insights and hunches, he frequently loses patience with his clowning and growls, "Go to hell!" He will, however, defend him against any and all threats and slanders. Once, in "Take It and Like It," an assistant district attorney labeled Kennedy a rat. "Call him a rat again, Rube," warned MacBride, "and I'll hit you with a radiator."

The final story appeared in the August 1936 *Black Mask*. Entitled "Deep Red," it featured Kennedy in the leading part as he helps MacBride solve a murder, exposes a crooked senator, and tells off an assistant D.A. This was also Nebel's farewell appearance in the magazine.

That same year MacBride made it to the screen. Warner Brothers bought "No Hard Feelings (*Black Mask*, February 1936) and used it as the basis for a fifty-seven-minute B movie called *Smart Blonde*. The captain got demoted to lieutenant and lost the *a* from his "Mac." Kennedy underwent a sex change to emerge as Torchy Blane. Glenda Farrell, the smart blonde, created the role. She'd played brassy reporters before—notably in *The Mystery of the Wax Museum*—and was capable of a rapid-fire delivery that equaled that of Pat O'Brien or Lee Tracy. She portrayed Torchy in seven programmers all told, with Barton MacLane as McBride.

Probably the closest thing to Winchell in the pulps, though a nicer guy, was Jerry Tracy. Theodore Tinsley wrote twenty-six stories for *Black Mask* in the thirties, all but one about Jerry Tracy. Small, dapper, and a "Broadway wiseguy," Tracy wrote a gossip column: "Harvey Smith, feed and grain impresario, and his wife, the former Claire La Tour, are ffft-ffft. . . . Mrs. Smith has left for Reno to establish legal residence. . . . It's a girl. . . ." Tracy was employed by a flamboyant Manhattan tabloid called the *Daily Planet*; Winchell was employed by a flamboyant Manhattan tabloid called the *Daily Mirror*. When Clark Kent came to town a few years later, he also went to work for the *Planet*.

Frank Gruber, in his sometimes far from accurate memoirs, maintained that while "Jerry Tracy was a Broadway columnist, a frequenter of night clubs and gay spots. . . . I don't believe Ted Tinsley was ever in a night club himself." Some months before his death in 1979, Tinsley told Will Murray, "As for Frank Gruber . . . I had small association with him, knew little of his professional or social life—and vice versa. His knowledge of me amounted to considerably less than zero." Tinsley's wife added that while he never enjoyed nightclubs, "he loved parties and we went to lots of them." His picture of New York newspaper, show business, and café-society life in the Depression years is a believable, though somewhat romanticized one. And Tracy ran into a great many more murders than Winchell ever did.

Although the little columnist had a nose for news, he had as well an affinity for showing up by chance just before a brutal murder or two. He could walk in any place from a Park Avenue mansion to the New York World's Fair, always "faultlessly attired," and the odds were in favor of at least one bloody corpse soon showing up. Tracy, more or less cooperating with his longtime pal from police headquarters, Inspector Fitzgerald, then set out to solve the case.

While slow to anger, the feisty Tracy would take only so much aggravation:

> Tracy's angry clutch almost tore the buttons from Huston's coat. He whirled the young lawyer around. His voice was low, almost conversational.
>
> "One more crack out of you and I'll hang one on your jaw!"

He was also not one to suffer slurs on his occupation:

> He heard a low, angry gasp from Lily Barker.
>
> "So that's who you are!" she said harshly. "Jerry Tracy! A cheap tabloid columnist! A keyhole snooper! A—a garbage collector!"
>
> "Right!" Tracy grinned. "With a proud record of always delivering the garbage. Never muffed a bum tomato in my life."

Another reason quite a few reporter characters appeared in the pulps is that quite a few pulp writers had once been reporters themselves. Ken O'Hara, of the *Los Angeles Tribune*, was one more of *Black Mask's* resident newsmen and he was featured in its pages, intermittently, from 1933 to 1947. The stories were by Herbert H. Stinson, who'd been a reporter on several big-town papers around the country. When asked to explain to the magazine's readers how he'd come up with O'Hara, Stinson replied,

I met the mugg originally back in 1931 when I was a police reporter myself. It was shortly after a very spectacular double murder, involving a political boss, an ex-newspaperman and a former deputy district attorney, had been sprung on the Los Angeles public. The cops arrested the killer but he beat the rap at his trial with a self-defense story that left lots to the imagination, at least to my imagination. So just for the fun of it, I doped out a story that filled in the hazy corners of the case. It was a natural, my job being what it was, to make my mastermind in the story a reporter instead of a cop.

Stinson went on to say,

That was the genesis of O'Hara. By special permission of the copyright owner, he was named after one of the most lovable and quickest witted Irishmen to ever grace the staff of the *Brooklyn Eagle*—God rest his soul. In personality O'Hara's a sort of combination of his namesake, of a big rough-tongued Los Angeles cop of my acquaintance, and of a New York City editor who once had the good sense to fire me. I like the guy and I like writing about him. Probably that's because he's just the sort of reporter I'd like to have been. When he wants to crash somewhere, he always crashes; whereas they used to throw me out at least fifty percent of the time.

The prolific Fred MacIsaac once admitted to having "for some years worked on Boston newspapers," initially as "a waterfront and police reporter." The detective he created for *Dime Detective* was far from being a proper and orthodox sort of newspaperman. Addison Francis Murphy, better known as Rambler Murphy, was a tramp reporter. A tall, thin redheaded young man and a first-rate investigator, he suffered from an incurable wanderlust. He'd drift into a town or city, usually having arrived by boxcar, and get a job with the local paper: "Murphy had earned as much as two hundred and fifty per week, and had accepted as low as fifteen." Because the Rambler had a knack for coming up with front-page stories, big metropolitan tabloids and small-town sheets always hired him. He stirred things up, solved murder cases believed unsolvable, got the goods on crooked politicians, put a local version of the Ku Klux Klan out of business. His trouble was, he just couldn't stay put, and the more successful he got on a job the more uneasy it made him.

There are seventeen stories about Rambler Murphy and they are among MacIsaac's best stuff. They're tough and realistic, well constructed, yet somehow sentimental and sad as well. The first of them, "Alias Mr. Smith," which appeared in the April 1, 1933, issue of *Dime Detective*, ends with the city editor of the *Boston Sphere* trying to persuade the Rambler to stick around:

> "You'll go on like this and die in a flop house some day. You're set for life on this paper. Get sense, will you?"
>
> "Some day maybe," replied Addison Francis Murphy with a far-away look in his eye. "Not yet. If anybody tries to get my address, you don't know what's become of me."

He shook hands with the editor and nodded pleasantly to the members of the staff who greeted him on his way out.

Gorman gazed after him until he had closed the door behind him, sighed, shook his head and then picked up a sheet of copy. "Ah, what the hell," he remarked and dismissed the Rambler from his mind.

The final story was "Object—Murder" in January 1940. Set in San Diego, it ends with Murphy having breakfast with the girl in the case:

"Frank, I suffered torture all the time you were on that yacht. I like Freddy but—but—I love you."

He stared at her hard. He patted her hand. "Kid, I'm a bum. I can't support a wife. I'm not a marrying man. Snap out of this. Here's your big chance. You deserve it—"

"You advise me to marry Freddy Graves?"

He evaded her gaze. He swallowed a lump in his throat. "Yes," he said. "Sure. It's the smart thing to do."

There were tears in her eyes. "All right," she agreed. "Now will you please get out of here?"

MacIsaac died later that same year.

George Harmon Coxe once said of his qualifications, "I'm quite sure that my only equipment for writing detective stories is something of a newspaper background plus an interest in crime." He'd apparently put in only a little time as a reporter. "I had worked around newspaper offices for four or five years in California, Florida and New York," he said in the pages of *Black Mask* in 1941, "and though much of my experience was on the business side, I had a fair idea of what made reporters and press photographers tick." His Flashgun Casey, as his name implies, was not a reporter but a news photographer. "I had been doing some mystery novelettes, and I had read a few having a reporter as the central character," Coxe explained. "The only trouble was that whenever a photographer appeared in such yarns he was seldom more than a foil for the more superior reporter. . . . So—I guess I thought it might be a good idea if I tried to do some stories about a camera, just to give the other side of the picture. Casey is the result."

The initial Casey story, in which he was a second banana, was "Return Engagement" in the March 1934 *Black Mask*. "Joe Shaw bought the first one and by then I was writing the second one," Coxe once recalled, "and I wrote and told him I was sending him the second one. He said, 'We don't want any more series characters,' but by then it was in the mail and he liked it better than the first one, and he said, 'Go ahead. I like the characters. Keep going.'" There were twenty-one Flashgun Casey stories in the magazine plus two serialized novels. The "number one camera on the *Express*" last appeared there in 1943. In his entry on Coxe in *Twentieth Century Crime and Mystery Writers*, J. Randolph Cox describes the stories this way:

> A Casey plot can be summed up as a triple conflict: Casey is after a news story in pictures, the opposition (the criminals) don't want him to get those pictures, and the police don't want him

to interfere. Casey's interference, of course, delivers the criminals to the police. Casey is a figure from American folklore—the sentimental tough guy—and this may account for much of his appeal.

Flash fared better in other media than did any of his journalistic colleagues. Knopf published five novels in hard cover, and Avon issued a paperback collection of short stories. The character was featured in three B movies, the first of which was *Meet Flash Casey*, starring perennial juvenile Eric Linden as a bouncy, clean-cut Casey fresh out of college. Much more successful was the radio show, *Casey, Crime Photographer*, which came to the air in the summer of 1943 and lasted until 1950. Considerably more lighthearted and set in Manhattan rather than Boston, it was written by Alonzo Dean Cole—with some help from Coxe—and starred Staats Cotsworth. A television show, just plain *Crime Photographer*, lasted a little more than a year on CBS in the early 1950s. Darren McGavin was one of the two actors to take a turn as Casey. Marvel published four issues of a Casey comic book in 1949–50, making him one of the few pulp detectives so honored.

Richard Sale recently told me, "Daffy Dill was my favorite character." Daffy was the most frequently seen star newsman of the pulps, appearing several times a year in *Detective Fiction Weekly* from 1934 to 1943. He was, according to Sale, "patterned not only after my own newspaper experience but after some real cynical pencil-pushers I knew. I worked briefly on the N.Y. *World-Telegram* and a lot for the *Pelham Sun*, Pelham, N.Y. The main point was to develop a series character so that you could make a living."

Joseph Dill was a brash, cynical columnist. He recounted his own adventures in a breezy vernacular style, as indicated in this sampling of opening paragraphs:

> When I came into the city room of the New York *Chronicle* I felt lower than a flounder's flatside, and I had a hangover that would have done credit to the old Romans of Bacchus' day. Breathing was an exertion, walking was torture, and living, that moment, was superfluous.

> It was a little after two A.M. on the hey-hey white way, and Dinah and I had just left the Hideaway Club and were on our way over to Leon & Eddie's, where we planned to see the Broadway souls and heels in action, when we ran into a guy named Black Mesa Dean.

> I was sitting at Moe Jackson's desk, banging away on a little feature about the duck who had laid a golden egg when the telephone buzzed and stopped me in my stride. A duck and an egg were not crime, of course, and I was out of my department, but as a matter of fact, Moe Jackson was home sick with a hangover and since he covered stories on everything from poultry to tropical fish and bird dogs, somebody had to do his stint and I volunteered.

The Dinah mentioned above was Dinah Mason, the light of Daffy's life. "Erstwhile blonde and beautiful nymph, who went to Alabama U., came to the big city to be a drammer critic, was promptly put to work on the New York *Chronicle* switchboard for a year or so, and finally had snagged a berth reviewing cinemas." She never got around to agreeing to marry him, but they were an item throughout the series:

> Dinah Mason does things to me. The wrong things. The things that are not good for my health. She gives me a ringing in my ears, not unlike the sound of wedding bells. When I see her, I get high blood pressure and black spots before my eyes. When I don't see her, I suffer severe melancholia and my appetite isn't good. You get the idea. Love.

Sale seemed to feel about Manhattan the way Robert Louis Stevenson and G. K. Chesterton felt about London. That it was a city full of wonders, capable of providing Arabian Nights adventures. Daffy, to be sure, got himself involved with the requisite number of gangsters, goons, gamblers, and grifters. Fairly frequently, though, he'd encounter one of those Arabian Nights things—a headless lady, a voice from the grave, a corpse that got up and took a walk. Daffy was an expert at solving murders, his method based on both determined detective work and his firm belief that "the hunch is mightier than the clue." He often lent a hand to his longtime friend on the homicide squad, Inspector Hanley. The Daffy Dill stories were the prose equivalent of the very good, very slick screwball mystery movies of the period.

A favorite of most *Detective Fiction Weekly* fans, Daffy usually got the lead spot in the magazine and frequently appeared on the cover. There were, however, a few who found fault and whose criticisms showed up in the "Flashes from Readers" section. One reader took Sale to task for the way Daffy continually razzed his editor, explaining that "City Editors are dignified and efficient. They want prompt service, respect and obedience. No foolishness tolerated." Another correspondent wrote: "Please ask the creator of 'Daffy' if he really believes a man can take a fine violin to pieces, put a gun in it, and then expect that a first violin in a symphony orchestra would not discover that something is wrong."

Throughout the summer of 1939 a controversy over Daffy's gun and Sale's alleged mistakes about firearms in general flared in the letter section. Finally Daffy himself responded to these various barbs, in a story entitled "Goodbye, Gravescratcher" (*DFW*, September 23, 1939). He's seated in the Press Bar when some of his peers begin to chide him that his gun doesn't even exist, "that there ain't no such animal." A smug reporter says, "I've been reading some of your stuff, you know, your behind-the-scenes stories in that magazine you write for. They got a letter department in the back, and it looks like some of the boys have been taking you over the coals." Angered, Daffy "took out the .31 gravescratcher and threw it on him. It is no myth. There isn't a better balanced gun in the world, to my liking. The stock is fitted into the hand beautifully, and the barrel is full of hand-worked scrolling. The only thing I ever had against my boothill campaigner is that it fires too small a bullet. I bought it cheap in El Paso, Texas, when Candid Jones and I were going through there once, fast." The .32 Colt dragoon pistol, by the way, is destroyed in that story and Daffy is forced to use other weapons from there on.

A spin-off of the series was started in the late 1930s. This featured Candid Jones, fotog on the *Chronicle* and sometime cohort of Daffy's. Candid, who also recounted his own adventures, was big and redheaded, tougher and less of a wise guy than his colleague. He went around more heavily armed, too—"I used to pack a Luger, a camera, and another small caliber gun concealed in a small movie camera which I strapped under my right arm." He'd been a Pinkerton operative, then an insurance investigator for nine years, and as his own *DFW* series developed he quit the newspaper to become a free-lance commercial photographer and private eye. Even back in his insurance days Broadway had been his beat. "Every stoolie, tinhorn and crook on the Gay White Way knew me," he explained. "They like to say on Broadway that Candid Jones had an iceberg where his heart should have been, and that ice-water ran in his veins instead of blood."

He usually dated a model named Claire Crosman, who "once told me I knew more people personally than anyone else in the world, and that every one I knew was either on the wrong side of the law or should have been there or would be there ultimately." Once, when a tough young woman pulled a gun on him, Candid passed along this bit of autobiography: "You see, lady, you never killed anyone in your life. And I think maybe you know that I've knocked off seven rats in my day. It takes a lot of nerve to shoot a man. You haven't got that nerve."

One of Candid's closest friends was Inspector Harry Rentano, of the homicide squad, and the two worked on several cases together. Like Daffy, Candid Jones had a fondness for crimes of an unusual nature. He dealt, for instance, with a murder that was apparently committed by a circus elephant, one that might have been perpetrated by a banshee, and one where the killer used Mother Goose rhymes as warnings.

He always got his pictures, solved his mysteries, and took no guff from anybody. In the story "Tip Your Hat" he goes to the rescue of a girl who's fainted on the dance floor of the Pelican Club. The hoods don't want him to do that, one of them warning him:

> "You're shooting off your mouth in the wrong place, bo. Now run along and peddle your papers before I wing you one."
>
> I said, "There's no reason why I should argue with you, is there?"
>
> "No," he said nastily. "Not a one."
>
> "Fine," I said, and hit him only once because it was a short sharp cross with my whole right side in it, and it drove him into the crowd until he finally hit on his haunches and then folded. My hand didn't hurt at all. It was a nice punch. He was cold.

An equal-opportunity tough guy, Candid treated lady crooks rough, too:

> I figured the dame with the gun for a rank amateur and I pulled a sandy on her. I took a flower pot off the fire escape and dropped it down into the yard. It made a sucking plop when it hit and it sounded faraway, but she heard it and turned her head to the window. It was the effect I wanted. She thought someone was in the yard below.

> She came over and opened the window while I
> clung to the wall outside. She cautiously eased
> her head over the sill and peered down, trying to
> spot the cause of the sound.
>
> I walloped her on the skull with the Luger
> barrel and she never even grunted. Just fell on
> the sill there like a baby.
>
> I took the .45 from her and climbed in.

In addition to the Candid Jones tales, Sale did at least one
about Timothy Barnes, who was the weatherman on the
New York Chronicle.

Over in *Popular Detective* he had a series running in the
mid-1930s about newshound sleuth Penny Packer. Packer
was a feisty fellow who covered crime for the *New York
Clarion.* He dated the receptionist on the paper, a
"brunette vision" named Connie Cole, and was a pal of
homicide cop Jim Scott. These yarns, as Sale confirms,
were actually Daffy Dill rejects recycled to a lesser-paying
market.

Far fewer female reporters showed up in the detective
pulpwoods. One who did was Katie Blayne, known to her
friends as the Duchess. She was an attractive, aggressive
young lady who worked the crime beat for the *Sun.* Her
adventures, which ran in *Detective Fiction Weekly* in the
mid-thirties, were recounted by a gentleman reporter from
a rival paper who had an obvious crush on the Duchess.
Whitman Chambers, another onetime newspaper man,
was the author.

"Journalism was a popular vocation for female secondary
characters in pulp series," points out Bernard Drew in his
anthology *Hard-Boiled Dames.* "Christine Stuart was a

reporter in the Candid Camera Kid tales in *Detective Novels*. Diane Elliot was a newshound in *Operator 5*. Betty Dale worked a beat in *Secret Agent X*, as did Doro Kelly in *Captain Zero* and Winnie Bligh in *The Masked Detective*."

There were numerous other newsroom detectives to be found in the pulps. Raoul Whitfield wrote a couple of stories with newspaper backgrounds for *Black Mask*, one about a down-on-his-luck reporter for *Argosy*. William E. Barrett, who graduated to writing best-sellers with religious themes, contributed a series to *Dime Detective* in the mid-1930s. It dealt with a column written by a fellow named Dean Culber: "The *Blue Barrel* with its automatic-pistol mast-head was the *Star's* exclusive feature; a slang column that had done for the world of crime what Winchell had done for Broadway. The chiselers and the double-crossers and the petty cheats feared it and when it leveled on a man, it rarely missed." The notion of a tough guy running a lovelorn column was utilized by Frederick C. Davis for fifteen novelets in *Dime Detective* in the early forties. Bill Brent—"there were two hundred pounds of him, including his size eleven brogans, his crooked nose, the cigar on which he was gnawing bitterly, and his sour disposition"—had been forced into fronting the *Recorder's* advice column and posing as Lorna Lorne, whom the public thought was "a grandmotherly dame whose kindly eyes gazed through rimless glasses delicately chained to a reel pinned on one sympathetic shoulder." Quite a few of the letters Brent received led him into violent murder cases.

Chapter 10

The Phantom Detectives

The most private of the pulp detectives were those who donned masks, costumes, or elaborate disguises to combat crime. Their true identities were known to few; their vigilante methods of solving cases were frowned on by the police. As outcasts and misfits with obvious identity conflicts they were tremendously appealing to adolescent readers of all ages. Most often the pulpwood titles showcasing the exploits of these mystery men far outsold those that offered the more realistic hard-boiled sort of material. Although they flourished most successfully in the Depression-ridden 1930s, their origins can be traced back to a much earlier period.

Masked men, bent on various sorts of revenge and retribution, had frequented the pages of cheap fiction publications in both America and England for much of the nineteenth century. Phantoms on both sides of the law were frequently to be found in penny dreadfuls, nickel weeklies, and dime novels. These characters appeared not only in urban settings but in the Wild West as well.

167

Professor Henry Nash Smith has pointed out that the familiar western "formulas had to be given zest by constant search after novel sensations. Circus tricks of horsemanship, incredible feats of shooting, more and more elaborate costumes, masks and passwords were introduced." The first two decades of this century saw the arrival of a variety of mysterious avengers in such other media as hardcover novels and silent films. These included the Scarlet Pimpernel, Fantomas, and the Lone Wolf.

In 1914, one of the earliest and most influential of the mystery men of the pulps appeared. Street & Smith's *People's Magazine* was where Jimmie Dale, alias the Gray Seal, made his debut. He was the creation of Canadian author Frank L. Packard. Inspired by such earlier cracksmen as Raffles and Jimmy Valentine, Jimmie Dale did them one better. He had an alternate identity, that of the Gray Seal, who skulked through the midnight streets of New York, masked and mysterious. Hunted by the police, but actually a man dedicated to justice, he struck swiftly and left behind only a small sticker, the notorious gray seal. In the everyday world Jimmie Dale was a wealthy playboy, and when he wasn't being the Gray Seal he had several other identities to use. "As Larry the Bat, the dope fiend, he slinks through dens of Chinatown," a blurb explained. "As Smarlinghue, the artist, he cadges beers in the Bowery, and as the Gray Seal . . . he uses clues and tips gathered in these disguises to battle and confound the underworld." The underworld was, as Robert Sampson points out in *Yesterday's Faces*,

> a major subject in Packard's work. Like the dime novelists, he reached into the streets for his

characters. His backdrops were immigrant-jammed slums, drinking dens, fetid alleys, the Old Bowery, the lower East Side, Chinatown. . . . The dime novels had superimposed melodrama, all purple-eyed in fiery robes, on familiar scenes of the day, described them tersely, rushed on. Packard, working in a more literary tradition, treated similiar scenes, similar character types naturalistically—realism (qualified) with strong moral overtones.

The leading manufacturer of phantom detectives and mystery men was a onetime newspaper reporter from the Midwest named Johnston McCulley. Even though he created one of the most famous masked men of the century, McCulley is little remembered and seldom written about. It was in the spring of 1919 that his serial *The Curse of Capistrano* began in Munsey's *All-Story Weekly*. This five-part story introduced Zorro to the world. While this was McCulley's best-known character, about whom he wrote over sixty novels and stories, Zorro was only one of the many dual-identity characters he created.

McCulley's chief market for this sort of thing was Street & Smith's pioneering mystery pulp *Detective Story*. In 1916, using the pen name John Mack Stone, he introduced a hooded villain called Black Star. "The stories were told from the point of view of those who opposed Black Star's plans," explains historian J. Randolph Cox. "It was the Fu Manchu/Nayland Smith situation." Next came another mysterious criminal known as the Spider, a very popular name for both villains and heroes. Gathered together, all the Spiders of pulps, movies, and comics would make for quite a convocation.

McCulley was also responsible for a string of masked good guys in the 1920s. Among them were the Thunderbolt, the Man in Purple, and the Crimson Clown. The Thunderbolt was in reality John Flatchley, "the only remaining member of an old and respected family." After returning from the Great War and learning that the fortune left to him by his uncle was illegally gained, he returns the money to the "poor dupes" whom his uncle and a group known as the Big Six have bilked. The rest of the group refuses to follow suit and "a couple of months later The Thunderbolt made his appearance." The police and the Big Six suspect that it's Flatchley who's robbing these financial scoundrels and redistributing the wealth. Yet no one can prove it or capture the elusive fellow who wears a "devilish black hood with the design on the front of it" and is "dressed in black, his hands covered with black rubber gloves."

As might be expected, the Man in Purple "dressed in shimmering purple from head to foot. He wore purple trousers, a purple coat that buttoned up close beneath his chin, purple gloves, and a sort of purple hood over his head." When not wearing the purple, he was a debonair man about town named Richard Staegal. Only his man Brophy knew that he spent his nights looting crooked business tycoons and redistributing their wealth. "I make it my business to run down such men as you and make them pay!" the Man in Purple explained to one of his victims. "I intend, whenever I find a crooked man like you, to take my toll of him!"

Delton Prouse was the "scion of a wealthy family" who

resided in a small penthouse apartment "such as many bachelors dream of having." He'd been an intelligence officer during World War I and was now known as "a cultured gentleman, courteous and debonair." Using his ability as a master of disguise, he often entered the underworld. "There, he mingled with crooks, whom he despised, studied them, learned their tricks and artifices and invented ways of circumventing them." Prouse was also an amateur magician. Most important, he was the Crimson Clown. In his later adventures he'd worked out a way of dealing with the nagging problem of changing in and out of his costume. "Beneath his shirt, on either side of his body, was a flat package so thin that only a careful search would have revealed it," McCulley pointed out in one adventure. "Each package was a crimson clown suit of thin opaque silk, chemically treated. Attached to each was a tiny vial containing a certain acid." Once the Clown was through for the evening, and before the cops caught up with him, he'd whip off the suit, pour the special acid on it, and watch it disintegrate. Somewhat less altruistic than his contemporaries, he always kept a percentage of the loot for himself.

Another prolific practitioner was Herman Landon. Born in Sweden, he came to the United States in his teens. Starting in 1902, he worked for newspapers around the country and by 1915 was managing editor of the *Washington Herald*. He eventually gave up news for fiction and provided *Detective Story* with two different mystery men, the Gray Phantom and the Picaroon. The Phantom borrowed his color and much of his M.O. from the Gray Seal. He enjoyed a number of identities, preferring most often to pass as a debonair man-about-town under such classy names as Cuthbert Vanardy and Allison Wyndham. An orphanage lad, he'd grown up on the streets and eventually graduated from street gangs to "a sinister preeminence in the underworld." Landon described him as "a rollicking Robin Hood" who was motivated by "a thirst for thrills rather than a desire for gain." Fairly early in his career he switched to fighting crime instead of perpetrating it. "It was rumored that a woman's ennobling influence had led the Gray Phantom's life into a more tranquil sphere." The woman was Helen Hardwick, a very trouble-prone lady who was forever getting herself kidnaped and otherwise jeopardized. She persisted in addressing her lover as "Phantom Man," which prompted him not to pop her one but to send her little gray orchids that he bred himself. A police lieutenant named Cullingore recurred in all the stories, engaged in a fruitless effort to end the Phantom's career.

Landon's other mystery man also owed a debt to Frank L. Packard's creation. Whereas the Gray Seal was in reality playboy Jimmie Dale, the Picaroon was in reality playboy Martin Dale. The Picaroon's chief occupation was that of gentleman cracksman, but in the course of his nocturnal exploits he usually managed to right wrongs, solve mysteries, and rescue damsels in distress. "Years ago he had been the victim of one of the law's blunders, resulting in an unjust conviction and incarceration," we are told, "and this was his revenge." He expected eventually to come to grief, "but in the meantime his career of a rollicking Robin Hood was giving him all the retributive satisfaction and thrills his nature craved."

The Picaroon was just about the only Robin Hood who pulled off most of his capers for the benefit of our four-footed friends. After making off with jewelry or other loot, he'd send a card to his wealthy victim. A typical one read:

> I trust you will pardon my little jest and excuse the liberties I have taken with your valuables. They will be returned to you as soon as you have donated ten percent of their value to the Society for the Protection of Animals.
>
> The Benevolent Picaroon

The cards used "a special kind of paper and a special style of engraving."

He didn't go in for any sort of flashy costume or mask. Using a "small, tumble-down dwelling in West Third Street" as a hideaway, Dale would retreat there to transform himself. "When the door opened again, the man who emerged was not Martin Dale, clubman and social favorite, but the Benevolent Picaroon. . . . He was an inconspicuous, slightly stoop-shouldered man, with a mild scholarly face and somber eyes." The Picaroon was frequently found in *Detective Story* in the 1920s, and no fewer than eight volumes of his exploits were published.

The biggest wave of phantoms came in the thirties. It was triggered, aptly enough, by *Detective Story*. In the summer of 1930, to promote the sales of the magazine, Street & Smith went on the air with a radio show called *The Detective Story Magazine Hour*. Initially an actor named James La Curto simply read a story from the magazine, but it was soon felt that the narrator ought to be given a mysterious name and the production beefed up. The name that was eventually agreed on was the Shadow. Gradually the program went in for more production, stories were dramatized, and La Curto took to talking in a hollow voice while he assured his listeners that "The Shadow knows." The Shadow was a modest celebrity in his own right and Street & Smith found they had, almost by accident, a new and popular character. They decided to turn him into a hero with a magazine of his own. To help on the project they hired an amateur magician from Philadelphia.

The young man was Walter B. Gibson, friend of, and ghostwriter for, such magicians as Houdini, Blackstone and Thurston. Gibson was working as a staff writer for the Philadelphia Ledger Syndicate and had written some for true-crime magazines. He had not read much in the pulp field when he was asked to take on the Shadow. But he had read the adventures of Jimmie Dale and most of the major detective fiction writers of the time. "I was particularly fond of Arsène Lupin," Gibson once told me. Lupin, the French superthief created in 1907 by Maurice Leblanc, specialized in intricate and audacious schemes and impenetrable disguises.

The editor whom Gibson first worked with was Frank Blackwell, whom he'd come in contact with while trying to sell to *Detective Story*. Street & Smith was cautious with its new pulp and planned *The Shadow* originally as a quarterly, telling Gibson if the first issue went over they'd hire him to write three more. He would be writing the Shadow as Maxwell Grant. The magazine was an immediate success and soon changed to a monthly and then, for a while, twice-a-month publication.

The Shadow wasn't an easy man to get to know. In the first novels, in fact, even Gibson doesn't seem quite sure who he really is. Unlike the Jimmie Dale novels, there are no interludes in the Maxwell Grant epic showing the real

Shadow relaxing with friends before slipping into a disguise. The Shadow never appears before the reader undisguised. Often he lurks in the background, more like the sinister villain of a movie serial. The Shadow novels, especially those of the early 1930s, are usually about the people he works on and through, the crooks he destroys and the agents he manipulates. Eventually the Shadow picked up an assortment of alter egos. His best-known alias was millionaire playboy Lamont Cranston. He also took to appearing as Fritz, janitor at police headquarters. Toward the end of the decade it was made known that the Shadow was actually a noted aviator named Kent Allard. By this time most people thought he was actually Lamont Cranston, including writers of the radio show and at least one of the authors who filled in on the magazine series.

An early and successful competitor of the Shadow was the Phantom Detective. A product of the Thrilling pulp works, the *Phantom Detective* magazine got under way in February 1933. The Phantom had become a detective chiefly out of boredom, a common complaint among rich playboys. "Born of wealthy parents who died when he was a child, Richard Curtis Van Loan had grown up under the competent tutelage of Frank Havens, millionaire newspaper publisher," explained an early novel. "But Van felt stifled by the smugness of the people around him and the sort of lives they led. He tried big-game hunting, deep-sea fishing, polo, other sports. All these eventually lost their appeal. He was bored—desperately, terribly bored." Service in World War I had cheered Van up, but then came the Armistice, and the same old Park Avenue ennui hit again. "It was during one of these periods that Van, at Frank Havens' suggestion, tried his hand at solving a minor crime that stumped the police. He was successful—startlingly so. And he found his true vocation at last. Hunting criminals, matching wits with them, supplied the element of danger and excitement that he craved. Richard Curtis Van Loan became the Phantom."

A master of disguise, the Phantom carried a small but incredibly stocked makeup case with him. It even had tiny lights for the mirror and held an endless supply of wigs and beards. He also brought along plenty of straight pins, for when he didn't have time to change clothes between disguises, he used pins to change the hang of his garments. Once, in turning from suave businessman to scruffy hood, he "used a few pins to give his clothing the appearance of careless fit and general disregard that would be characteristic of the new part he was creating."

For most of the saga, which lasted from 1933 to 1953, only Havens knew who the World's Greatest Sleuth really was. Even his daughter Muriel, who had a crush on both Van and the Phantom, took close to two decades to tumble onto the secret. Whenever Havens wished to summon the Phantom in a hurry, he caused a red beacon light atop the *New York Clarion* building to flash. On the occasion when the beacon was being repaired and the publisher was anxious to contact Van, he had the police commissioner turn all the traffic lights in Manhattan red for five full minutes. This caused the Phantom Detective to come running, but we were never informed how the city's quick-tempered motorists reacted.

Wearing either top hat and mask or one of his many disguises, the Phantom worked on well over 150 cases before he retired. These cases included "The Jewels of Doom," "The Death-Skull Murders," "The Corpse

Parade," "The Yacht Club Murders," "The Sabotage Murders," and "The Rubber Knife Murders." The first year of Phantom stories was credited to G. Wayman Jones and the dozens thereafter to Robert Wallace. Leo Margulies, editorial director of the Thrilling pulps, didn't remember how he made up the Jones name. But Robert Wallace came about because "Edgar Wallace was very big at the time." The probable creator of the series was D. L. Champion. Among the many other authors who ghosted the Phantom Detective were W. T. Ballard, Ryerson Johnson, Norman Daniels, and G. T. Fleming-Roberts.

The first artist to illustrate the cases was Mel Graff, who was laboring in the art department of the Associated Press's Manhattan offices at the time. In 1935 he began drawing a daily newspaper strip called *The Adventures of Patsy*. It seems likely that his earlier association with the Phantom Detective inspired Graff to introduce a character named the Phantom Magician to *Patsy*. This latter phantom has the distinction of being the first masked and costumed crime fighter to appear in comics.

In the summer of 1933 Popular Publications got into the mystery man field with *The Spider*. Billed as "a new magazine with a dynamite punch," the ten-cent monthly featured a novel entitled *The Spider Strikes* in its maiden issue. In his first adventure the Spider behaves in the accepted Jimmie Dale manner, but instead of gray seals, he leaves behind seals featuring "a reproduction, in blood-red, of a particularly hideous spider." In everyday life the Spider is Richard Wentworth, world traveler and New York clubman. "You'll love Richard Wentworth, once you meet him," promised ads. "And you'll love the one woman in all the world who shares his deadly secret—Nita Van Sloan.

You'll get to like his quiet Hindu servant, Ram Singh."
Along with the long-suffering and unsuspecting Inspector
Kirkpatrick, this was the running cast. The first two Spider
novels were the work of R. T. M. Scott, a Canadian author
who was mainly known for a series of books and stories
about a character called Secret Service Smith.

The problems Scott gave the Spider to cope with were,
by pulp standards, pretty prosaic. A master criminal in the
first one, a gambling joint in the second. But bigger and
better struggles were in store for Wentworth. Commencing
with the December 1933 issue a new name was signed to
the novels. Grant Stockbridge, with its echoes of Maxwell
Grant and staid New England towns, was the pen name
now in use. It was used almost exclusively by the prolific
Norvell W. Page. According to his publisher, Page would
"show up at the office with a black cape and dark slouch hat,
wearing a Spider ring." His friend and colleague Theodore
Tinsley added to this view: "Norvell's personality was not
subdued. At times his flamboyant cape suggested he might
be a Bolshevik, with a small bomb concealed for socially
corrective action. Actually he was a nice guy, with a yen
toward theatrics." Not only did Page share his hero's
passion for dressing up, he seems to have identified closely
with him. To a fan who tracked him down by mail he
admitted, "I can not any longer conceal from you the fact
that the Spider's other name is . . . Norvell W. Page!" It
was his feeling that the novels served a moral purpose. "I
know that the Spider actually helps people," he said. "That
there are those who appreciate his idealism, even though it
is expressed in violence. . . . My editors agree with me
that the Spider should stand or fall as an agency for good."

Under Page the Spider graduated to bigger and better,

often cosmic, troubles. Even the titles of the monthly novels became more startling: *Wings of the Black Death, The Serpents of Destruction, Satan's Death Blast, The Devil's Death Dwarfs, The Claws of the Gold Dragon*. The Spider takes to dealing with "a city swept by Bubonic Plague," with an epidemic that turns America's finest families into a "set of swanky thieves and killers," with the Emperor of Hades, who "scattered his scarlet, slaying devil-dust" over New York, with five thousand mad dogs who are rampaging in Cologne, Ohio, and with dozens of other equally upsetting problems.

In the Page version Richard Wentworth takes to roaming Manhattan in a "ruthless and terrible" disguise. His nose, "altered by putty, became hawklike and predatory. His lips disappeared, so that his mouth was a gash. False, bushy brows, a lank, black wig. . . . A black jersey covered his formal shirt, a cape for his shoulders, a broad-brimmed black hat." This Spider was considered so horrific that, while he could be viewed in interior illustrations, he rarely was allowed on the covers of the magazine. To sell the magazine on respectable newsstands the Spider wore a domino mask and was obviously a handsome chap underneath it.

The magazine ceased during the Christmas season of 1943. Norvell Page, perhaps not surprisingly, considering his gift for imagining vast conspiracies and his faith in the effectiveness of virtuous violence, had gone into government work in Washington, D.C., shortly before that.

Mystery man fever also struck the industrious, market-conscious Erle Stanley Gardner in the early 1930s. He produced several series of masked avenger and phantom investigator novelets, mostly for the Munsey pulps.

Detective Fiction Weekly featured both the Patent Leather Kid and the Man in the Silver Mask; *Argosy* housed the Roadrunner and a pair known as White Rings. A practical and fairly realistic man, Gardner was not always completely at ease with heroes who donned masks before getting down to their detective chores. In his White Rings stories, for instance, the two avengers take their name from their "black masks with the weird white rings around the eyes." But Jax Bowman and Big Jim Grood, who do business out of an office complete with pretty secretary, strive to wear their masks as little as possible. They use them usually only to scare gangsters, whisking them off whenever they have to deal with ordinary civilians.

More flamboyant was the Man in the Silver Mask, who starred in three *DFW* yarns in 1935. An introductory blurb explained him this way: "His past and his face are unfathomable mysteries, but the world knows and the underworld trembles at his terrifying and amazing deeds." Aided by a seemingly sinister Oriental named Ah Wong, the Masked Man was headquartered in a secret hideaway and was fond of kidnaping gangsters and threatening to torture them. His war against crime was basically psychological and he and the deaf-and-dumb Chinese never actually followed through on their threats. Sometimes merely a look at the Masked Man was enough to scare the average crook into talking:

> There was a suggestion of grim, sinister firmness about the mouth, a suggestion which was heightened by the firm chin. The eyes were a peculiar slate gray. The upper part of the face was concealed by a mask of metallic silver, modeled to

conform to the contours of the nose, but not entirely concealing the cheek bones and the lower forehead. From behind the mask, the gray eyes seemed to take on the metallic glint of the silver.

The Patent Leather Kid came by his name originally because of his glossy shoes. Later, though, he took to wearing a mask—"a mask of shiny patent leather." He also wore a dark suit and black silk gloves while on the prowl. Gardner had used a character of this name in a single story in *Clues* in 1930, but the true, longer-lived Kid made his debut in *Detective Fiction Weekly* in the spring of 1932 and appeared there thirteen times over the following two years. This kid was Dan Seller in real life, seemingly yet another wealthy playboy who loafed around his club and spoke with a lazy drawl. "The period of transition by which Dan Seller, the wealthy club man, became The Patent Leather Kid, a mysterious and romantic figure of the underworld, was by no means simple," explained Gardner. "It involved the use of three taxicabs, two complete changes of apparel and the occupation of three different rooms in as many hotels."

At the ultimate hotel the Kid shared a bulletproof penthouse with a tough sidekick named Bill Brakey. Brakey, who frequently donned a mask and went along on the raids against crooks and corrupt politicians, was a walking encyclopedia of underworld lore. When, for example, an innocent ex-con had been framed for a jewel heist, Brakey knew at once who the real culprits were—"Shucks, it was a play made by Slick George and Baby Faced Edna." Another of the Kid's aides was Gertie, the hotel switchboard girl. Presumably she eventually left his employ to go to work for Perry Mason.

Like his creator, the Patent Leather Kid was a champion of the underdog and could never rest while an innocent man was unjustly locked up. Not entirely altruistic, he always managed to turn a profit while serving the cause of justice. Usually he'd keep half of any cash or loot that passed through his hands. The Kid dealt in somewhat more sophisticated capers than masked contemporaries such as the Shadow and the Phantom Detective. He left the archfiends and the criminal masterminds to them, favoring gangsters, crooked cops, and dishonest businessmen. He did go in for disguise, though, once even smearing on blackface to become a railroad porter. He was also considerably more lighthearted than his peers, and the traps he set, while always leaving the guilty caught, had aspects of practical jokes. Gardner had no high opinion of the nameless city where the Kid operated, showing its police and elected officials as more than willing to railroad the innocent, accept bribes, and badger witnesses. Few saw it that way, but the Kid was a definite civic asset.

The Roadrunner, who didn't wear a mask or costume, was nevertheless a fairly mysterious figure. Also known as El Paisano—Spanish for roadrunner—he did his stuff in five *Argosy* novelets from 1933 to 1935. This was long before Chuck Jones appropriated the fleet-footed desert bird for Warner Brothers cartoons. Gardner's character was an American who prowled the border between the United States and Mexico. He had "earned his nickname from the peculiar habit which he had of appearing almost simultaneously in various places along the border." His fight against evildoers was helped not only by the fact that he moved fast but because of "his uncanny ability to see in the dark." The company that was formed to turn out the first

Perry Mason television show, by the way, was named Paisano Productions.

Another fellow who could see in the dark was the Black Bat, who started appearing in Thrilling's *Black Book Detective* with the July 1939 issue. The Bat was an impatient representative of law and order who went in for vigilante shortcuts. In real life he is Assistant District Attorney Tony Quinn. Once Quinn had been blinded by "certain crooks in a mad effort to destroy evidence." The world still believes Quinn blind, but, thanks to a secret eye transplant, "not only can he see perfectly, but—he can see in the blackest darkness. To him, even pastel shades are visible in a jet black room." As a D.A., Quinn "fought crime and criminals with the relentlessness of the full majesty of the law—which can groan and creak at times." And so Quinn felt compelled to hurry things along as the Black Bat, "a man who prowled the night as noiselessly as a wraith, and whose name brought respect and fear from the most hardened criminal, and a man to whom many of the police who admired him—but not all—were grateful. The Black Bat fought criminals with their own methods. Ruthless, with a disregard for the law, he made his own rules as he went along. Here was a man who could fight with fists, or guns or knives." In what may be a coincidence, the Black Bat appeared on the stands very soon after the similarly garbed and motivated Batman. The Black Bat held forth in *Black Book* from the July 1939 issue until its final one early in 1953.

As the decade of the forties began, another batch of mysterious detectives broke into print. The most successful of these, relatively speaking, was the Green Lama. He began in the April 1940 issue of *Double Detective*, a title that had been around since 1937. The Lama's premier novel-length excursion was entitled "The Case of the Crimson Hand," and Richard Foster was listed as the author. Foster was actually Kendall Foster Crossen, who was editing *Detective Fiction Weekly* for the Munsey outfit at the time. "The Green Lama came into existence in a sort of offhand manner," Crossen once told me. "*Double Detective* wasn't doing too well and they wanted to flesh it up. . . . It was finally decided to do something to compete with the Shadow and I was asked to draw up an outline for such a character. The result was the Green Lama (first called the Gray Lama but changed for reasons of color on the cover) and I was asked to write it."

Like the Shadow, the Lama had several alternate identities. The Shadow would sometimes be wealthy playboy Lamont Cranston, and the Green Lama would sometimes show up in Manhattan as wealthy playboy Jethro Dumont. Dumont, as was frequently mentioned in the footnotes accompanying the novels, "had fallen heir to a fortune estimated at ten million dollars while still at Harvard. It was during his college days that he first became interested in the Oriental religions. Shortly after his graduation he went to Tibet and studied in the Lamaist sect of Buddhism. He then returned to America and took up residence on Park Avenue."

When he was being Dumont, the Lama had an Oriental servant named, possibly as a nod at the then-popular Dorothy Lamour movies, Tsarong. Another of the Lama's cover personalities was that of Dr. Pali, the name deriving from the name for the sacred language of the early Buddhist writings. With the aid of his small makeup kit the Green Lama was able to assume "the ruddy, moon-like" face of the doctor. In this phase he wore a dark green suit, light green ecclesiastical shirt, and turned collar. To appear as the Green Lama he wore a green hood and robe over his other clothes, with a braided-hair ring in the six sacred colors on the middle finger of his right hand. Around his neck he wore a dark red *kava*, or scarf, which was his only weapon. He appeared in fourteen issues and sank with the magazine early in 1943.

Included among the other colorful ops were the Green Ghost, the Masked Detective, the Purple Scar, the Man in the Red Mask, and the Black Hood. By this time they had to compete not only with their still active predecessors but with the ever-increasing number of costumed crime fighters who were setting up shop in comic books. Playing it safe, the Green Lama branched out into *Prize Comics* and the Black Hood went to work in *Top-Notch Comics*. Both fared better there than in the pulps.

Chapter 11

Screwballs, Oddballs, Etc.

Not every private eye was hard-boiled. The pulps made room for a diverse array of other sorts of detectives—soft-boiled ones, eccentric ones, sinister ones. Fat men, midgets, misers, acrobats, cracksmen, tattoo artists, mystics, wise guys, magicians, crackpots, hypochondriacs, canines, hemophiliacs, blind men, and bookies were among the sleuths to be found solving cases and catching crooks in the pulpwoods.

The leading producer of odd and unusual investigators, from the 1920s through the 1930s, was Erle Stanley Gardner. His earliest was Speed Dash, who began his career in Street & Smith's *Top-Notch* in 1925. Besides being what a blurb called a "versatile and amazing detective," Speed was a human fly, capable of scurrying up the sides of buildings with the greatest of ease. Gardner got the idea for this series when he saw, on a windy day in the spring of 1923, an agile gentleman scale the First National Bank Building in Ventura, California. Since Gardner had his law office on the top floor of the building, he got a good view of the whole thing. "When the Human Fly climbed the First National Bank Building at Ventura and passed the hat to the applauding audience on his descent," he later explained, "I promptly conceived the idea of having a human fly as the hero of a mystery story."

Richard "Speed" Dash specialized in unusual and perplexing cases and charged impressive fees. He kept himself always in tip-top shape:

> The profession of human fly is the most dangerous profession in the world, bar none. Demanding strength which must be abnormal, requiring sinews of steel, it also needs nerves that can never fail. The human fly trains his fingers to have a gripping strength which will crush a raw potato into liquid; trains his hands and feet to coordinate perfectly, and then ascends the sheer sides of perpendicular buildings, gripping for support only those ornamental, architectural irregularities which are usually found in all lofty structures.

The stories caught on with the readers, many of whom were juveniles, but the editors insisted that Gardner make it perfectly clear that "Speed Dash led a *pure* life. The things he did could only be done by one who had never inhaled the faintest wisp of tobacco smoke, never touched his lips to a beer glass or looked at a woman's neatly turned ankle." Speed's popularity increased and, according to Gardner, he was requested to make his acrobatic detective even more pure. Many years later he confessed:

> I did the best I could. On one occasion, Speed Dash was spilled out of an airplane high above the

Grand Canyon while the villain was descending
in a parachute. Speed swooped down on the
parachute in a free fall, latched onto the villain,
survived the fall, and found himself at the very
bottom of the Grand Canyon at a place where the
perpendicular cliffs were towering thousands of
feet above him. The villain, who had not lived a
pure life, was trapped, to his own destruction,
but Speed Dash, who had crushed his raw
potatoes that very morning, worked his way up
the Grand Canyon and emerged triumphantly at
the top.

In all, twenty Speed Dash stories ran in *Top-Notch*, the
final one in 1930. The initial one was called "The Case of
the Misplaced Thumbs," and that was the very first time
Gardner used the title format that was to serve him so well
on his Perry Mason novels.

Much less active than Speed, and even cleverer, was
Lester Leith. Besides being a crime solver, he was a
cracksman, a thief, and a consummate con man. Like an
expert conjurer, Leith could divert and misdirect both
crooks and cops while he went about his work. He was, as
Ellery Queen pointed out, "the Robin Hood of detectives
who solved baffling mysteries in order to crack down on the
cracksmen. Instead of robbing the rich to help the poor,
Lester Leith robbed the crooks 'of their ill-gotten spoils'
and gave the proceeds to deserving charities—less '20
percent for costs of collection.'" It's my opinion, by the way,
that his last name should be pronounced exactly like the
word "lithe." A writer who would christen a daredevil
Speed Dash and a D.A. Ham Burger wouldn't be above a
punning name for his lithe and debonair hero.

While as carefully and cleverly plotted as Gardner's best straight detective yarns, the Leith adventures were out-and-out comedies. The hero's attitudes and life-style burlesque those of the more serious amateur cracksmen and playboy sleuths from Raffles to Philo Vance, a fact that Lester Leith himself was fully aware of. Several set pieces figured in the series, which began in *Detective Fiction Weekly* in 1929. Most of the tales opened with Leith at ease in his suite:

> Lester Leith, his wellknit, athletic form encased in silk pajamas and lounging robe, tapped the end of a cigarette on the arm of the reclining chair. His slate gray, inscrutable eyes were lazy lidded with the amusement of one who finds life a very enjoyable adventure.

> Lester Leith sprawled out in indolent ease. Attired in a lounging suit of white silk, he seemed immune to the heat, which had persisted unusually late in the season.

> Lester Leith, slender, debonair, gathered the lounging robe about him and sprawled at silken ease.

Soon after that we are filled in on the setup of the household:

> Standing slightly behind the chair, six feet two of ponderous servility, Edward H. Beaver, the bullet headed individual who acted as his valet,

regarded the lounging form with eyes that were dark with hatred.

The police strongly suspected that Lester Leith financed the huge, charitable trusts, which he had created for the benefit of the unfortunate, by utilizing his chain lightning mind in beating the police to a solution of some of the more spectacular crimes which were reported from time to time in the newspapers. The police contended that, once having determined the identity of the criminal and the hiding place of the loot by means so baffling in their ingenuity that the detectives had hitherto been unable to follow his mental processes, Leith, or some other mysterious hijacker, deftly stripped those criminals from their ill-gotten gains and left them dazed, and defenseless, struggling in the toils of the law.

Beaver, who was in reality a police undercover man, had been planted in the service of the suspect as a valet for the purpose of directing Leith's attention to certain crimes which the police considered good bait. . . . That Leith's ingenuity had so far enabled him to steal the bait while the authorities helplessly jerked on the string, did not lessen the perseverance of the officers.

The fun in these escapades was in watching Leith solve the mystery, divert the loot, see that justice was done, and elude the police completely. His schemes always involved improbable props and personnel and were often so intricate that only Rube Goldberg would have been able to diagram them. The schemes most often got under way with Leith's instructing his valet, whom he persisted in calling Scuttle, to round up an unlikely list of paraphernalia and people, as, for example:

"Scuttle," he said, "do you know anything about zircons?"

The valet's tone was choked.

"You mean the stone that looks so much like diamonds?"

"Yes."

"I know a little about them."

Leith regarded the tip of his cigarette.

"Get me some, Scuttle. Get them from one of the wholesale gem shops. Get odd shapes, if possible, so the stones can be identified. And you'd better get a bill of sale to them. Then you can buy me a microscope, a tray, two test tubes, a phial of iodine, and a little corn starch, some empty bottles, and a magnifying glass. And then, Scuttle, I'd like to have a pair of handcuffs that won't lock."

Lester Leith chuckled and said chidingly, "Don't be so damned mercenary, Scuttle. Go and get me one of the best vacuum cleaners on the market. Get me an assortment of cameras and quite a few films. Also get me some books on photography."

Lester Leith's eyes narrowed slightly. "Scuttle," he said, "I'm going to want a rope of pearls—a

cheap synthetic imitation of the rope which was
stolen, and I'm going to want a skullcap with a
luminous button on the top, and I'll want some
cold cream and a small quantity of powdered
graphite."

Even though the law, as represented by the slightly
dense and easily excitable Sergeant Ackley, always knew in
advance, thanks to the treacherous Beaver, what Leith was
gathering together in the way of trappings, be it a "glamour
girl" or a Chinese mandarin's skullcap with a button atop it
that glowed in the dark, they were never able to outfox
him. That cap, for instance, Leith was able to persuade a
jewel thief to don. Then, by convincing him they were
under siege in a pitch-black room, got him to run to his
hidden safe. Ackley and Beaver were incapable of anti-
cipating stratagems such as that.

Gardner remained devoted to Leith for nearly fifteen
years, producing over sixty novelets about him. Leith went
on hiatus in 1937, returning the following year but in a
different magazine. After seven capers committed in *Detective Story* he returned to *DFW* in the autumn of 1939. In
1943, the last year that Gardner contributed to the pulps,
the only two characters he wrote about were Ed Jenkins
and Lester Leith. *Ellery Queen's Mystery Magazine* began
a series of six reprints in 1950. Gardner said in an
introduction:

A lot of slush has been written about the pulps,
principally by writers who knew the market only
by hearsay. It is true, as has been so frequently
charged, that the better pulp writers, being paid

by the word, ground out a terrific wordage. They were able to do this, however, only because they had imagination. The telling of the story may have been crude, but the writers always had a story to tell. Characters may have been sketched with broad strokes. There was certainly no time for subtlety. But the writer of that period either had ingenuity, imagination, and a touch of novelty, or he went broke. Lester Leith was a typical character of the pulps, and written for the pulps. The Leith stories were batted out at a terrific speed in a white heat of creative imagination, and they were popular.

Many other out-of-the-ordinary detectives were batted out by Gardner in his pulp days. He even produced a sort of Leith simulacrum in the person of the audacious Paul Pry. This alliteratively named fellow made over twenty appearances in *Gang World* and then five in *Dime Detective* from 1930 to 1939. For *DFW* there were Sidney Zoom and Senor Lobo, for *Dime Detective* Dane Skarle and Small, Weston & Burke, and for *Double Detective* Ed Migraine, alias the Headache.

Lester Dent ran Gardner a close second when it came to the manufacture of offbeat private eyes. In fact, none of his many detectives in the pulps of the thirties came anywhere near being conventional. Even when Dent pretended to do a routine hard-boiled dick, the character turned out wild and wacky. Take, for instance, Curt Flagg, a tough American op who somehow held forth in Dell's *Scotland Yard*. "Wildcat" was the first of three Flagg novelets—billed as "A Thrilling Book-Length Novel of the Oklahoma Oil Fields and Gun Law"—and was featured in the March 1931 issue. Like many of Dent's heroes, Flagg is a giant of a man. He has "a pair of hands the size of gallon pails." Employed by a New York–based agency, he's been summoned to Tulsa on a case. The story opens with his getting into trouble on a rooftop:

> It takes big, thick fingers and tremendous strength to clasp a man's face with one hand, seize his throat with another, and break his neck.
>
> Private Detective Curt Flagg grunted and strained with the effort.
>
> There was a rotten sound in the cold winter darkness of the rooftop, like an eggshell collapsing. The body knotted in a convulsive death jerk. The gun in the fellow's hand exploded, stabbing flame into the ink void.

The case involves a murder frame, a kidnaped Indian girl, and millions in oil money. Flagg is not especially bright, but he wins out simply because he's indestructible. Early in the story he realizes he's been shot:

> Curt released his belt and unbuttoned his trousers. With fingers that could palm half dollar pieces and bend them into half moons, he explored the furrow across his hip. The gash was ugly, deep enough to hold a broom handle, but was already sealing with its own blood. He rolled his handkerchief into a cylinder, laid it in the wound, and buttoned his trousers again.

That done, he goes on with his investigation. A while later a young lady stabs him:

> The hand held a nail file, amber handled, with a tapered steel blade as long as a stiletto.
> The blade hit a rib, glanced—and tunneled under the skin for six inches like a big splinter.
> Curt chopped at her temple with the edge of his hand. The blow traveled something like six inches and knocked her unconscious instantly.
> He dragged the sliver of steel out of his side, looked at the fragments of flesh embedded in the file grooves, and pitched it under the second of the two single beds.

Naturally Flagg could dish it out, too:

> He ducked instinctively as the gun roared in his ear. He felt the plucking sensation of a bullet tearing through his coat. Then he planted his feet, swung the gunman once about his head and let him fly.
> The fellow screeched in terror as he felt himself hurtling through the darkness. The screech died in a horrible, splashy sound. The sound a handful of mud makes when it is dropped on cement, or a rock.

Dent turned his attention to scientific detectives next: Lynn Lash in *Detective-Dragnet* in 1932, Lee Nace in *Ten Detective Aces* in 1933, and Foster Fade, the Crime Spectacularist, in *All Detective* in 1934. All these investigators were extremely tall and fond of gadgets. Their caseloads were similar to those Doc Savage would handle, involving sinister rays, white-hot corpses, aroma assassins, and other off-trail problems. Finally, in 1937, Dent invented the best of them—Click Rush, the Gadget Man.

Clickell Rush was a tall, wiry young man who was particularly fond of the color brown. "His suit was business brown, his eyes brown, his hair brown, and the watch on his right wrist had a brown band." He was a dedicated inventor of gadgets for catching criminals and solving crimes and a very reluctant private eye. He came to the big city "with the notion of selling super-modern, crook-catching gadgets to the police." The cops, however, dismissed him as a crackpot. Initially no one but a toad took him seriously:

> The toad was about of a size to sit in a small washtub. It was ugly green on top, mud yellow underneath, and had warts. It was made of papier-mache on a brass frame, and contained a small but very good wired radio "transceiver."
>
> The wired radio in the toad could communicate with another "transceiver" when both outfits were plugged in on the city lighting system.

The toad was activated by putting a lighted light bulb in its mouth. The thing was mysteriously delivered to Rush in his first exploit in *Crime Busters* (November 1937). Along with it came half of a ten-thousand-dollar bill. The toad introduces himself as "Bufa, of the species Bufonidae, which feeds on snails, slugs, insects, and such undesirable things." Bufa was anxious to hire "an expert private detective to investigate crimes I think need solving." Click points out that he's not an expert private eye, but the talking toad insists that he wants him for the job. The promise of getting the other half of that bill is enough to goad Rush into a new career. The anticrime toad has a somewhat mean-minded sense of humor and enjoys razzing his employee. When the $10,000 fees no longer prove sufficient to get Click Rush rolling, Bufa does such things as framing him for a crime and thus convincing him it's to his benefit to solve the mystery. Bufa's true identity remains forever a secret to the Gadget Man, and to the reader as well.

Dent let his sense of humor out of the closet on the seventeen Gadget Man stories he produced in the late thirties, managing to blend hard-boiled action with screwball farce. Many of the titles were strange and provocative—"The Little Mud Men," "The Remarkable Zeke," "The Hairless Wonders," "The Devils Smelled Nice."

Of all the many prolific pulp writers of the period, nobody could open a story any better than Dent. And with the Click Rush yarns he was especially inventive:

Clickell Rush changed mustaches.

The man who was collecting noses didn't have a nose himself.

The block of stone was about five feet long, two feet wide, and a foot thick. It probably weighed over a ton.

It fell fifteen stories and missed Clickell Rush by the length of an arm.

* * *

It was not six white horses when it started. It was six white pigeons.

To make it simpler, it started with one white pigeon. There was even some doubt about whether the pigeon was white. Because it was dark nighttime when the man ate it.

The man obviously did not eat the pigeon willingly. He ran into a hospital at two o'clock in the morning, screamed, "I ate a pigeon! Get it out of me!"

Before he was thrust into the P.I. trade, Rush had already invented over a thousand gadgets. No adventure went by in which he didn't use at least a few of them. Most often he carried several large trunks of stuff with him. These contained the larger gadgets, such as his portable X-ray device, his phone-tapping equipment, and his bullet-proof vest. He would also distribute a lot of smaller gimmicks throughout his clothing. These included a re-peating hypodermic needle that could be strapped to his upper arm under his shirt and used to deliver doses of a knockout drug; a pack of exploding matches; containers of knockout gas that could be attached to his knees under his trousers and activated by knocking his knees together; and a small container of liquefied tear gas that could be concealed in a secret compartment in the heel of his shoe. Dent never came anywhere near to cataloging all of Click Rush's thousand and some inventions, but he several times allowed him to express the wish that "the gimmicks were not so silly and fantastic, so that he could sell them to some metropolitan police force for a nice piece of change."

Dent had been writing these stories under his own name. By 1938, thanks to the success of Doc Savage, his pen name of Kenneth Robeson was much better known to Street & Smith readers. Editor John Nanovic suggested Dent try a second series for *Crime Busters*, announcing its advent with a bit of fantasy of his own:

> Many of you wanted Kenneth Robeson, author of the Doc Savage novels in "Doc Savage Magazine," to be added to our list. We had to take all these letters to Mr. Robeson to convince him that he should do some stories for us, but now he's convinced and you'll be seeing Kenneth Robeson's stories. The first will appear in the next issue. Mr. Robeson gave us his word, just as he was sailing for Europe on the *Queen Mary* the other day, that the first yarn would be in on time!

Just as wacky as the Gadget Man tales, the five adventures of Ed Stone attributed to Kenneth Robeson dealt with another reluctant private eye. A sometime prizefighter and usually broke, Stone finds himself saddled with a mysterious Chinese valet called One. Functioning somewhat like Bufa, One pushes Stone into cases and sees to it that dough is collected. In his short career Stone got tangled with such things as Shakespeare's remains, beached whales, and a trailer truck named the Dancing Dog. Dent came up with some nice openers on these stories, too, especially on "The Horse's Egg," which commences:

> The boy stood on the burning deck. He was not being brave about it, however. He was jumping

up and down and hollering at the top of his voice—yelling that he didn't deserve to die, that he had never done harm to anybody, that he couldn't swim. He could be heard at least a mile.

Among the many other distinctive ops was J. Paul Suter's Horatio Humberton, who appeared in *Dime Detective* in the early 1930s. He was a part-time dick and a full-time undertaker. "Though Horatio Humberton earned the principal part of his living by the direction of funerals," it was explained, "another science, the study of crime, was much nearer his heart. When it came to embalming a murdered man, he could do a good job; but he would be far more enthusiastic in the task of finding the murderer."

Dime Detective was also the home of William E. Barrett's Needle Mike, a St. Louis tattoo artist who doubled as a sleuth. Actually Mike was a millionaire playboy who'd created an alter ego, a "self that went adventuring into the grim fringes of the underworld when life amid luxury became too boring to be endured."

Another investigator with an unusual occupation was T. T. Flynn's Mr. Maddox. A resident of *Dime Detective*, the heavyset Joe Maddox was the "smartest bookie operating." His profession required him to visit racetracks all across the country and every visit got him involved not only with the ponies but with murder. There were thirty-five stories in all, including "The Devil's Derby," "Blood on the Blue-Grass," and "Post-Mortem at Pimlico." They ran from 1938 all the way to 1950.

Another pulp that was hospitable to oddball investigators was *Detective Fiction Weekly*. Therein you'd find the likes of the already mentioned Daffy Dill and Lester Leith as well as Jigger Masters. Aside from his first name, there was nothing especially odd about Jigger Masters himself. He was a typical private detective of the stalwart, heroic school and possessed a "grave, craggy countenance." Author Anthony Rud saw to it, though, that Masters worked on some very unusual and unsettling cases. These included "The Stuffed Men," "Terror Cave," and "The Riddle of the Severed Finger." In this last one his client is a young lady who, in searching for her missing uncle, finds the dregs of a rather sinister meal in his living room: "There, hooked around the handle of a teacup on the tray was a long, slender, spatulate finger detached from its hand and body! It was the index finger of a man!" An even more interesting repast was featured in "The Feast of Skeletons." As the blurb put it to anxious *DFW* readers, "What did it mean, that banquet hall in the tomb, where the diners were human skeletons?" Human skeletons, Rud informed us, "clad in dinner jacket, shirt, collar and tie." The scene made for a memorable cover painting.

Arthur J. Burks was one of the most popular and prolific of pulp writers, turning out every sort of story for every sort of magazine. It should come as no surprise that he wrote about unusual detectives. One such was Harlan Dyce, head of the Dyce Detective Agency. He was "but three feet tall and weighed sixty pounds." During his circus days he'd been billed as General Midge. Dyce stories ran in *Clues* and then *Detective Yarns*.

The oddest detectives of the decade were those who plied their trade in shudder pulps like *Dime Mystery* and *Strange Detective Mysteries*. Horror fiction, thanks mostly to the efforts of publisher Harry Steeger, enjoyed a brief heyday in the thirties. Considerably nastier than the pioneering *Weird Tales*, these pulps—as well as other newcomers like *Horror Stories*, *Terror Tales*, and *Uncanny Tales*—offered sex and sadism along with their chills. In the late thirties private detectives, most of them weird and flawed, were added.

According to Robert Kenneth Jones in *The Shudder Pulps*, it was *Strange Detective* that kicked off the short-lived defective detective trend in its first issue, dated October 1937. "Norvell Page led off the issue, sporting the title: 'America's No. 1 Master of the Extraordinary Mystery Tale.' His hero, Dunne, was an expert at ju-jitsu, which of course, stood him in good stead. He had unusual quarters, rigged with chairs that slid forward by themselves, and a talking cigar box—guaranteed to disconcert the visitor. In the same issue, Paul Ernst's Seekay sallied forth." He was the more unusual of the two, "because Seekay had no face. Where a face should have been there was a blank curve of something pink and softly shining, like celluloid, extending from the hairline down to a point just under where a chin should be." Ernst went on to explain, "Through this half cylinder of plastic substance that shielded Seekay, stared black eyes that were like jet with little fires in them. Over the gruesome shield was thick, virile black hair shot with gray streaks. Under it was a tall, powerful body immaculately clad in gray spring flannels. . . . What dreadful disfigurement did Seekay hide under the half-cylinder of celluloid?"

A year later, with its October 1938 issue, *Dime Mystery* converted to a weird crime fighter policy. An editorial, reports Jones, "hailed the new type of story as something 'brand new in the entire field of magazine fiction,' overflowing with 'all the eerie menace and weirdly terrifying atmosphere, plus speed, dramatic punch, plot complication and breathless tempo of the best detective mysteries.'" Included in the *DM* lineup were John Kobler's Peter Quest, whose investigations of weird cases were hampered by periods of unpredictable blindness; Ejler and Edith Jacobson's the Bleeder, a hemophiliac op billed as "the world's most vulnerable dick"; Bruno Fischer's Ben Byrn, who had withered legs but an enormously powerful torso. Among Byrn's cases were "Flesh for the Monster," "Prey for the Creeping Death," and "The Dead Hand Horrors." Fischer wrote the Byrn stories under the pen name Russell Gray and in the late 1930s was, as he once told me, "the top man in the field." His top rate for horror yarns was one and a quarter cents a word. "In a period of three years, ending with the beginning of the war, I wrote around a half million words a year and sold every word."

Various civic and legal pressures across the country, including a vigorous campaign waged in New York City by feisty, odd-shaped Mayor La Guardia, helped put an end to most of the weird pulpwoods by the early 1940s. La Guardia felt he had the responsibility to keep pornography off the newsstands of Manhattan and he believed most of the horror pulps as well as the Spicy types—especially their steamy covers—were borderline pornography. "La Guardia wouldn't let them in," reports Jones, "unless the covers were removed, and they were sold under the counter." Even the more sedate pulp publishers didn't like them, since many of the attacks spilled over to cover all the pulps. The Munsey Company, for instance, ran editorials in 1940 distancing themselves from pulp-paper magazines "on whose covers you see half-clad women being tortured or attacked by deformed caricatures of men—or the enactment of some perverted crime depicted in terrifying detail." The Munsey folks didn't advocate censorship, although they did agree with law enforcement agencies that "these magazines are a decided factor in crime; that unbalanced, perverted individuals read them and are incited to violence; that even young children can buy them on the newsstands and be easily led to attempt to duplicate what they read." It would have been a bright and inventive kid who could've duplicated most of the goings on in the terror tale pulps, but nonetheless this view was commonly held by many critics. In place of censorship or suppression, Munsey suggested "a house-cleaning job to be done by the readers and the publishers." This is more or less what happened. It's possible, too, that the real horrors of a new world war dampened interest. At any rate, the bulk of the horror pulps left the stands. With them died the bizarre branch of the private-eye field. More conventional odd and eccentric P.I.'s, though, continued to proliferate, and in the forties, the last full decade in which pulp magazines were to flourish, many new ones showed up.

Chapter 12

A Hearse of a Different Killer

As the 1940s began there were still dozens of pulp detective titles available on the newsstands. Although Hammett, Whitfield, and Nebel had long since left the pulps, and Chandler, Sale, and Gardner would follow in the early forties, many of the writers who'd broken into the pulps in the previous decade were still around—such as Norbert Davis, H. H. Stinson, D. L. Champion, and Roger Torrey—and new writers emerged, including Fredric Brown, Richard Deming, William Campbell Gault, Merle Constiner, and John D. MacDonald. World War II brought on paper shortages, mailing delays, and other problems for publishers. The first successful digest-size detective fiction magazine was launched in the forties. The number of series characters increased, and editors, perhaps in an effort to boost morale with a little humor, took to sticking more and more punning titles on the stories. Some notable examples of this trend were "You're the Crime in My Coffin," "Man's Best Friend Is His Murder," "Booty and the Beast," "A Stiff in Times Saves Nine," "Cheese It—the

Corpse," "Slugs Along the Mohawk," "Rhapsody in Blood," and "Open the Morgue, Richard!" This was to be the last full decade of the pulps, though few suspected it at the time.

The United States officially entered World War II in December 1941, and within a short time signs that there was a war on began to show up in the pulpwoods. An editorial in the *Black Mask* for April 1942 explained:

> Roger Torrey's story in this issue was purchased and scheduled for publication about a month and a half before Pearl Harbor and indicates some of the difficulties a monthly magazine encounters these days in trying to give its readers fiction with current timeliness. 'Tain't all skittles and beer figuring out how to keep abreast of developments when the whole picture has a habit of shifting overnight. Maybe we'd better just stick to gangster stories laid back in the Prohibition era, and forget things as they are.

That same issue carried an ad for gift boxes for servicemen. Popular Publications was putting up the boxes, which contained "articles of standard merchandise—items not issued by the government—needed, used every day by men in the services." The $2.98 "oodle box" held such items as razor blades, a toothbrush, hair tonic, shoe polish, and copies of *Adventure*, *Big Book Western*, and *Big Book Detective*. Slogans took to appearing under the stories: "Back Our Fighting Men—Buy War Bonds!" Also seen were public-service ads:

Waste Paper Is A Weapon Of War!
Made Into Cardboard Containers For Food,
Ammunition, Supplies, It Carries The War To
Our Fighting Fronts—And To The Enemy.
Save Paper—And Save Lives By Helping To
Shorten The War!

The number of pages in the pulps gradually dropped
from 128 to 112 to 96. Since in most cases the type size was
reduced, the word count remained about the same, and
some magazines maintained that "it has been possible to
adjust the type size in such a way as to give the readers in
the fewer pages even more wordage than before." As the
war progressed, publishers also took to running notices
apologizing for magazines that arrived late: "We regret
that, due to the difficulties of wartime transportation, your
magazine may sometimes be a little late in reaching you. If
this should happen, your patience will be appreciated.
Please do not write complaining of the delay." The cover
price on many detective pulps, including *Dime Detective*,
was now fifteen cents.

For the most part publishers remained optimistic during
the war years. From 1940 to 1945 roughly three dozen new
mystery pulps were introduced. One of the more successful titles was Popular's *New Detective*, which appeared in
1941 and emphasized writers—such as Bruno Fischer,
Frederick C. Davis, and G. T. Fleming-Roberts—rather
than series characters. Its motto was a modest "The Best in
Crime Fiction!"

In the summer of 1940 the Trojan Publishing Corporation—one of the many names of the folks responsible for
both *Spicy Detective* and Superman—had brought forth

Super-Detective. During its early years the pulp devoted most of its space to novels featuring Jim Anthony, a Doc Savage impersonator—"He's Indian; He's Irish; and He's All-American!" The Anthony chronicles were credited to John Grange, which was an alias for the team of Robert Leslie Bellem and W. T. Ballard. Anthony left *Super-Detective* after the October 1943 issue and it converted to hard-boiled fare.

Ziff-Davis Publishing, located in Chicago, was apparently not bothered by paper shortages. It had been publishing the two fattest science fiction magazines in the world—*Amazing* and *Fantastic*—and in the spring of 1942 added *Mammoth Detective* to its line. An average issue consisted of 272 pages and included "an 80,000 Word Book-length Novel" as well as ten or so short stories and a grab bag of departments and features. Among its authors were Frank Gruber, Robert Bloch, and the dependable Bruno Fischer. William P. McGivern wrote his first detective story for *Mammoth*, and Howard Browne, under his John Evans pen name, first wrote of his Chandler-inspired private eye, Paul Pine, for the magazine. Browne also served in an editorial capacity. *Mammoth Detective* sold for twenty-five cents and stayed alive until 1947.

The venerable Frank A. Munsey Company had begun the decade with what was either enthusiasm or a fatalistic attempt to go out with a bang. It introduced, all in the early months of 1940, *Famous Spy Stories*, *Detective Dime Novels*, and *Red Star Mystery*. The spy pulp printed recycled Max Brand stories and novelets. The hero of the dime-novel magazine was an old gent named Doc Harker, who ran a medicine show and doubled as a criminologist. The pulp became *Red Star Detective* with its second issue and expired after its third. *Red Star Mystery* made it through four issues. Its resident character was magician-detective Don Diavolo, also known as the Scarlet Wizard. Amateur magician Clayton Rawson wrote his adventures under the pen name Stuart Towne.

Munsey's *Double Detective*, as previously noted, was not especially helped by the addition of the mysterious Green Lama to its lineup. It fell early in 1943. In the early 1940s *Detective Fiction Weekly* ceased to be a weekly and became a monthly, calling itself *Flynn's Detective*. The magazine's dimensions ballooned to bed-sheet size, and the page count dropped to 64. There was little fiction to be found, the emphasis being on "True Crime Mysteries," as touted on the cover. But during this period Woolrich's *Phantom Lady*, under the title *Phantom Alibi* and without his William Irish pen name, ran as a six-part serial. Waiting six months to find out if the poor guy beat the murder rap must have heightened the suspense considerably. The Munsey Company went under as 1943 began. Henry Steeger bought *Flynn's Detective* and kept it going for another year and a half as *Flynn's Detective Fiction*.

The majority of the established detective pulps, however, did fairly well in the forties. Even *Spicy Detective* stayed in business, although it changed its name to *Speed Detective* in 1943 and cleaned up its prose and pictorials some. *Detective Story* continued strong. By the time it converted to digest size in the autumn of 1943, the editor was Daisy Bacon, the lady who'd made Street & Smith's *Love Story* magazine into a best-seller. *Black Mask* became part of the Popular Publications empire in 1940 and was edited for most of the decade by Kenneth S. White, who also edited *Dime Detective*. White brought new writers into both titles and encouraged some of the older ones.

Notable among this latter group was Norbert Davis, who produced a total of twenty stories for the two magazines from 1940 to 1943. A gifted and relatively successful pulp writer, Davis was handicapped, especially in the 1930s, by having a sense of humor. W. T. Ballard, who once told me that Davis "was as close a friend as I ever had," said that Davis never did that well with *Black Mask* in the thirties. "Although Shaw said that he could write the best letter of anyone in the business," Ballard explained, "his stuff was too whimsical to fit well into the action pattern." Davis fared better in the early forties. He sold a batch of stories to *Black Mask*, including three about John Collins, a somewhat abrasive army intelligence man whose usual cover identity was that of a boogie-woogie piano player. It was for *Dime Detective*, though, that Davis created two of his best series characters. First, starting in the February 1940 issue, came William "Bail Bond" Dodd and then, in July 1941, Max Latin.

Dodd was a bail bondsman, a profession that kept him in touch with a wide assortment of lowlifes, deadbeats, crooks, and eccentrics. Though he now and then visited the haunts of the rich, Bail Bond Dodd—which he was called only in editorial blurbs—was usually found in cheap saloons, run-down boardinghouses, and dingy civic buildings, the parts of the world where those on the fringe are to be encountered. The eight Dodd novelets are like scenarios for first-rate B movies, containing not only action, violence, and a mystery puzzle but wisecracking dialogue and a goodly supply of appealing character people. Dodd, like many of Davis's detectives and lawyers, looks quite a bit like Davis himself—"a big man, tall and loose-jointed, with deceptively wide shoulders." Ballard once described

Davis to me as being "a big man, standing several inches over six feet, a very gentle man who never knowingly hurt anyone." Dodd, the one sane man in the madhouse, solved most of his cases simply to make sure he wouldn't have to forfeit the bail money he'd put up.

Max Latin was featured in five *Dime Detective* novelets. He was a bit different in appearance from Davis's usual lanky heroes:

> Latin was wearing a tailored blue topcoat and a dark blue rolled brim hat, and he blended into the shadows as though he belonged in them. He was thin and a little above medium height, and he had a blandly confidential smile that didn't mean any more than the ones they paint on kewpie dolls. His eyes were greenish and tipped a little at the corners, and they never smiled at all.

He was the owner of a restaurant, though few knew it, where he hung out and could be consulted at his special booth. Guiterrez, a vainglorious chef who pretended to be even nastier than he really was, fronted for Latin and acted as the proprietor. Guiterrez "looked like a shadowy Satan with a stomach-ache" and lived for but two things—to cook up masterpieces in his kitchen and to insult all and sundry, including Latin. Although frequented by the best people in Southern California, the restaurant was basically a dump:

> Besides its food, the restaurant certainly had no other attractions. It was bare and dingy and crowded and noisier than a street fair on Saturday night. A mangy horde of waiters banged and

slammed around and swore at each other and the customers. The cash register clanged and a juke box shrieked in agony from one corner.

Latin enjoyed a reputation for being on the crooked side, but he was actually a relatively honest man. The idea that he was on the wrong side of the law helped him in his detective work, making it easier for him to get information and to move about in the shadier parts of town. As David Geherin notes, "Behind the mask Latin is a responsible member of the private eye fraternity."

In 1943 two hardcover mystery novels by Davis, *The Mouse in the Mountain* and *Sally's in the Alley*, were published by Morrow. These starred the incomparable detective team of Doan, a pudgy private eye with the soul of a con man, and Carstairs, a Great Dane who was the canine equivalent of Guiterrez. They'd appeared once before in a two-part novelet in *Argosy* in 1940. Nineteen forty-three was a good year for Davis. He virtually left the pulps to concentrate on slicks like *Collier's* and *The Saturday Evening Post*, selling to these impressively better-paying markets for the next several years. One more Doan and Carstairs story appeared, in *Flynn's Detective Fiction* in 1944, and a third novel was issued as a paperback original by Handi-Books in 1946.

Things began going wrong for Davis in the late forties. Early in 1949 he wrote to his friends asking for loans to keep going. According to Raymond Chandler, "he says he has sold one of fifteen in the last year." Ballard told me that "he wrote up until a few weeks of his death, but the market was changing. In fact, although none of us recognized it at the time, markets like the *Post* and *Collier's* were in deep trouble." Ballard also speculated that "the thing which shook Bert Davis and caused him to lose his sense of direction was the deaths of his two agents. First Phil Conroy, who had shared his progress from his first pulp sale, died, and then a few years later his partner Sid Sanders, who had handled all of Bert's slick-paper sales, also died. Bert simply never really recovered from the two deaths."

Mystery historian John L. Apostolu has done a great deal of research into Davis's life and death, and in Vol. 15, No. 1 of *The Armchair Detective*, he gave an account of Davis's last days:

> Early in that year [1949], Davis moved from Southern California to Connecticut. . . . That summer, for what reason I do not know, Davis made a trip to Harwich, Massachusetts. The town of Harwich is on Cape Cod, not far from the Kennedy family compound. It was in this resort setting that Davis, apparently despondent over career difficulties and other problems, took his own life.
>
> According to the death certificate on record at the Massachusetts Division of Vital Statistics, he ran a garden hose from the exhaust pipe of his car to the bathroom of the house in which he was staying. In the early morning of July 28, Norbert Davis died, at the age of forty, from the inhalation of exhaust gases. His body was cremated in Boston, and burial of the ashes took place at Inglewood Park Cemetery, near Los Angeles, on August 11.

Davis had died without leaving a will. In a document filed two months after his death, his estate was estimated at five hundred dollars.

D'Arcy Lyndon Champion had been writing for the pulps since the early 1930s, but usually not under his own name. Using the pen names G. Wayman Jones and Robert Wallace, he wrote many of the early Phantom Detective novels. As Jack D'Arcy he hit several of the lesser pulp detective markets with undistinguished short stories. An Australian by birth, he settled in the United States while quite young and served in the British army during World War I. Noted for being a whimsical man in private life, and a master of conning money out of editors—Leo Margulies being one of his favorite targets—he never displayed much humor or ingenuity in his pulp work until the late 1930s. Then he began writing as D. L. Champion. The work he signed his right name to was, most often, clever, hard-boiled, well plotted, and admirably screwball. Champion took the basic setup of the Rex Stout novels, that of an eccentric detective with a tough and not too admiring Watson, and came up with several very entertaining variations.

By the early 1940s he had a number of series going in *Dime Detective* and *Black Mask*. The most serious stories were those in *Dime Detective* dealing with Inspector Allhoff. Champion did over two dozen of those from 1938 to 1945. Considerably lighter and funnier were the adventures of a penny-pinching private eye named Rex Sackler. Sackler, whose cases were narrated by his junior partner, Joey Graham, had first practiced his profession in *Detective Fiction Weekly* in the late 1930s. Starting with the July

1940 issue, he set up shop in *Black Mask*. The twenty-sixth and final Sackler story ran in the January 1950 issue.

Joey Graham was not quite as bright as Sackler, who was described in blurbs as "the No. 1 money-grubber of all time" and "unchallenged world's champion penny-pincher." Joey was continually struggling to get a raise, to keep from having Sackler hoodwink him out of the paltry salary he did pay, and to solve a crime before his skinflint boss did. Rarely did he succeed in these ambitions, and this colored the way he described Sackler and the cases they worked on:

> Sackler's affection for money made Abelard's love for Heloise a tawdry and unimportant thing. Despite the fact of his commanding enormous fees, he lived like an indigent immigrant. He bought a suit only after his bare knees came peeping through the threadbare material. His hat was a blob of shapeless felt that I'm certain some doting uncle had awarded him on the day of his grammar school graduation. His shoes were odd lot three dollar bargains. But there was nothing shabby or cheap about his bank account.

> Sackler was smoothing out a rumpled morning newspaper preparatory to reading it. I knew from the journal's condition and previous experience that he had snatched it up from the floor of the subway, a procedure that enabled him to stash away another three cents along with the rest of the Sackler fortune.

> Our visitor sat down. Sackler watched him with
> his omniscient eyes which, I will swear, could
> stare right through a man's coat and into his
> wallet.

Although exasperating, miserly, and arrogant, Rex Sackler
was a very efficient private detective, and he was able to
solve the most complex mysteries with ease and not the
slightest trace of modesty.

Mexican private eye Mariano Mercado was a hypochon-
driac with a fondness for flashy haberdashery. Despite all
his foibles, he was, like Sackler, a shrewd and effective
investigator. Champion, who knew Mexico firsthand, produced eight novelets about the south-of-the-border sleuth
for *Dime Detective* from 1944 to 1948. For other pulps he
invented a detective who was a professional gambler, and
he attempted two separate series about midget private
eyes. After the pulps faded away, Champion turned to
writing true crime articles and an occasional paperback
novel. He died in Manhattan in 1968 at the age of sixty-
five.

The novelets about the Dean that Merle Constiner wrote
for *Dime Detective* also dealt with an eccentric investigator's adventures as narrated by his partner. Dean
Wardlow Rock, though, for all his erudition, was a very
tough detective, and Ben Mathews usually had nothing but
admiration for him. The initial story, "Strangler's Kill," ran
in the August 1940 issue, and by December 1945 eighteen
more had appeared. The titles got somewhat more intri-
guing as the series progressed—"The Riddle of the Bashful
Ghost," "Parade of the Empty Shoes," "The Affair of the
Bedridden Pickpocket." Constiner, as he once told me, had

a master's degree from Vanderbilt University, "where I minored in medieval history, to show you how far you can wander in this vale of uncertainties." He embarked on a full-time writing career in 1938.

Once in every story Ben explained the setup:

> Wardlow Rock is a private investigator who knows how to make money. We run a play that really brings in the results. The boss tells fortunes as a front and has an under-the-rose connection with the police commissioner. The Dean's a simple-acting duffer and strangers write him down as strictly foggy. There are those, however, that have a different view of the matter. You should see him with a burr under his saddle. He carries a shoulder-gun in a holster as big as a carbine boot—and likes to use it. The strangest thing about him is his hobbies. He has a hundred accomplishments from paper-making to fletching. Me, I just know two things—guns and locks.

And at least once there was a shoot-out:

> The ragged man snapped a slug through the cuff of my sleeve and I went down behind my belt buckle and got out the old bulldog. Why they picked me first, I didn't know at the time; later I realized that the Dean had them scared silly, they didn't much know what they were doing. Reggie let loose three times—once at the Dean and twice at the girl. He was just swinging his gun on me when the Dean got out his Magnum and touched

it off. Reggie's head was twisted back on his shoulder in his excitement and the chief's soft-nose caught him in the V of skin which lies just under the chin. His arms fanned out in a spasm of reflex and he went over chairs and little tables like a drunken man in a pile of milk bottles.

The Dean dealt in murder cases, but they always had odd elements. He enjoyed impressing clients with his arcane knowledge:

"You asked for it," the Dean said. "So I'm going to give it to you. Oneiroscopy, the study of sleep images and their interpretation, is one of the most ancient of all branches of prophecy. Flammarion, the astronomer, Aristides the magnetiser, Plutarch and Cicero, are only a few of its distinguished exponents. The Egyptians considered dreams as communications from the goddess, Isis. Thylbus holds that their predictive value is overrated . . ."

For *Black Mask* Constiner wrote of Luther McGavock, a private eye who was headquartered in Memphis and worked on strange and wondrous cases across the rural South. The eleven McGavock novelets were as full of odd lore and quirky characters as those about the Dean, and they featured Constiner's odd, dark humor. Absolutely no one, including the detective, was completely trustworthy, and McGavock's investigations were enlivened by, in addition to bloody murders, many intricate bluffs, lies, and deceits on the part of all involved. Some of the small

backwoods towns of the tales are as nasty and inbred as any
of the weird New England hamlets that H. P. Lovecraft
celebrated. "I was born in the village of Monroe, Ohio,"
Constiner once explained, "but lived much of my life
elsewhere. Yes, I lived a slew of years in McGavock's
South."

Shrewd though he was, McGavock couldn't seem to
figure out how to be likable:

> McGavock was a small man, wiry and tough. His
> coarse black hair was cut in a short pompadour
> and there was a tweedy sprinkling of gray about
> his temples. He had a taunting, selfish quality
> about him that aroused instant animal antagonism
> in total strangers. At some time or other he'd
> been with about every major agency in the
> country. A genius at getting results, he was a hard
> man to take. He'd never felt at home until he'd
> hit this Memphis outfit.
>
> His employers liked what he brought in but
> didn't want to know too much about his methods.
> He worked under a roving license—an agreement
> that the agency could repudiate if things got too
> hot. This one-sided arrangement was a constant
> gripe to him.

The summonses to attend a client were usually unusual.
Once McGavock was sent off to a benighted southern town
because his boss received a telegram reading, "Send best
employee immediately. Believe things critical. Am con-
vinced we have a zwanziger in town." Only in Constiner
stories did you find clients who knew that Anna Maria

Zwanziger was a nineteenth-century German poisoner. Another case commenced when a prospective customer wrote a letter stating, "I find myself suffering from a mild but irritating condition of abaction and would appreciate it if you would send a man here to alleviate it." Once a fellow sent a bottle of sawdust to get the agency interested in his case; another wrote to complain he had tramps in his girls' dormitory. No matter what the lure, McGavock was certain to get tangled up with a murder or two once he arrived at his destination. The last McGavock ran in January 1948. In the 1950s and early 1960s Constiner, according to his own account, "was in general circulation magazines mostly, *Collier's*, the *Post*, *American*, *Cosmopolitan*, and others." He wrote several very good, very individual western novels in the sixties as well, most of them paperbacks for Ace Books.

Ken White encouraged many another private-eye series for his twin detective pulps in the early and middle forties. Robert Reeves wrote seven novelets and a novel about Cellini Smith, a member in good standing of the Hollywood screwball school, for *Black Mask*. G. T. Fleming-Roberts, a prolific writer of pulp fiction, turned in a very enjoyable series of light detective novelets about Jeffrey Wren for *Dime Detective*. Wren ran a magic shop and doubled as a solver of seemingly occult mystery cases. Roberts even cast the lead role and usually mentioned that Wren looked like actor Edward Arnold. Arnold would have been a good choice had anyone made a Wren B movie, having already portrayed Nero Wolfe and Captain Duncan Maclain on the silver screen. H. H. Stinson created Pete Rousseau for *Dime Detective*. Dale Clark came up with Plates O'Rion and Highland "High" Price for *Dime*

Detective and Mike O'Hanna, a house dick in a Southern California resort hotel, for *Black Mask*.

Without doubt the most unconventional writer of pulp detective stories in this decade was Fredric Brown. Only infrequently did he do a story about a hard-boiled private eye or a tough cop, yet he appeared over a hundred times in such magazines as *Detective Fiction Weekly*, *Popular Detective*, *Detective Tales*, and *New Detective*. (He only showed up once in *Black Mask* and not at all in *Dime Detective* during this decade.)

Brown fashioned New Arabian Nights tales, using the slums of Chicago and the sleepy small towns of the Midwest as his settings. He was very much fascinated with the violence and madness that can be lurking in the shadows, or even in bright sunlight. In Brown's wonderland the Jabberwock sometimes triumphed, but other times he suggested there was still the possibility of finding love and fortune. In Brown's stories you got murders and robberies, but also a killer who dressed up in a Santa Claus suit and an innocent man who must find some dancing sandwiches to save his life. Like Woolrich, Fredric Brown sometimes abandoned hope, and some of his tales are hard-boiled in a different way from those of most of the other 1940s practitioners. Brown could be hard-boiled enough to say that there were no answers to some questions and no possibility of salvation. Fortunately he was gifted with a very strong sense of humor, which usually won out over the darkness.

Born in Cincinnati, Brown was a college dropout and spent the Depression years working as a proofreader and at various other printing jobs. He was in his early thirties when his first story, "The Moon for a Nickel," was published in the March 1938 *Detective Story*. He was residing in Milwaukee at the time and was a member of a local writers group. They put him in touch, in 1939, with a New York literary agent named Harry Altshuler, who has said:

> He sent me three or four short stories aimed at the detective-mystery field which was broad and vigorous at the time. But as he explained in a covering letter, he thought the best chance for quick sales would be in the "spicy" area. . . . I sent all those stories back to Fred with comments I meant to be helpful, telling him there was a big broad field out there and he was heading the wrong way by trying to work for this narrow segment. I did this, I recall, with a distinct feeling of regret, because I thought he had something on the ball, and I was sure he'd cling to his own notion and I'd never hear from him again. I was surprised, pleasantly, when he came right back with more stories. They looked good to me and I began pretty quickly to sell his work to the Street & Smith magazines, *Detective Story*, *Clues*, etc. and the Munsey group as well: *Detective Fiction Weekly*, *Argosy*, etc.

Brown sold frequently to the fantasy and science fiction pulps as well, magazines such as *Astounding*, *Weird Tales*, and *Unknown Worlds*. The September 1948 issue of *Startling Stories* featured his best science fiction novel, *What Mad Universe*. Brown's first novel in hard cover was

The Fabulous Clipjoint in 1947. He became fairly successful as a writer of books and the eventual demise of the pulps
didn't hurt him as much as it did others.

Another author who blossomed in the forties, and in
some unlikely places, was Roger Torrey. After 1942 he
ceased to be a contributor to either *Black Mask* or *Dime
Detective*. Daisy Bacon, who'd assumed editorship of
Detective Stories in 1942, made room for several of the
hard-boiled detective writers, including Norbert Davis,
William Campbell Gault, Carroll John Daly, and Frank
Gruber. "I stayed with Roger Torrey in spite of the protests
from the business department about his money habits," she
once told me. "Because of this, many editors also backed
down but I always thought his stories made it well worth
contending with. Of course he and I had an interest in
common in that we were both concerned about the welfare
of animals. I always thought that he and Jonathan Latimer
had a good old-fashioned down-to-earth touch with sex that
a good many of the other tough writers lacked."

Torrey, as usual, wrote about Irish detectives for Miss
Bacon. Among them were Hannigan, Clanahan, John
Ryan, and Shean Connell. Connell, a refugee from *Black
Mask*, shared a piano-playing ability with his creator and
sometimes undertook undercover jobs that involved his
posing as a cocktail-lounge or theater pianist. Connell is
also the detective in Torrey's only novel, a 1938 paperback
entitled *42 Days for Murder*. He had a practical view of
show business, and a Connell story about movie people
begins, "Everybody in the show worked for Supreme and
the whole bunch were as screwy as toads."

Torrey's novelets and stories, whether in the first
person or the third, are told with a matter-of-factness, an

acceptance of the world as far from perfect. His various Irish operatives are pretty good at perceiving their world as it is and making their way through it. They aren't noble or particularly cynical, but simply pragmatic. The detectives share a similar attitude toward women. Their notion is that dames are usually either venal or dumb. That's the way it is and you'll get along better with them if you just accept the fact.

The list of markets for Torrey's work dwindled, but *Private Detective* and some of its sister pulps bought a great many stories from him. With the exception of an op named Jenson, all of them used yet another batch of Irish detectives—Pat Mullaney, Pat O'Leary, Pat Malone, Riley Keenan, and, again, John Ryan. Torrey sometimes also used John Ryan as a pen name. The stories in *Private Detective*, *Super-Detective*, and *Speed Detective*, many of them set in Florida and the South, are tough in a weary, resigned sort of way. Not surprisingly, considering Torrey's alcoholism, most have scenes in saloons, nightclubs, and hotel cocktail lounges. His detectives are usually transients, stopping at a hotel or a rooming house while working on a case. Nothing shocks a Torrey detective, not brutality or sudden death or civic corruption. In a story called "Stake-out Kill" private eye Mullaney and his crew are on a case in the town of Rockville, which he describes this way:

> Rockville was and is a funny town. Saint Paul used to be one. Detroit used to be one. New Orleans used to be one. All were safe towns. A thief could come in, do a little paying off, and as long as he minded his business he'd be left alone.

He couldn't pull any local jobs—he had to keep his nose clean. . . . A nice arrangement for everybody. The cops had a few extra bucks in their pockets—something that always gladdens a policeman's heart. The citizens had a good safe town.

When one of his operatives is gunned down by a crooked cop, Mullaney just goes over and waits in the cop's backyard that night:

And then he came in, running the car into the garage and swearing as he stepped out of it.

By that time I was at the side of the place and I let him close both garage doors before I stepped out into sight.

I said: "It's me, Lieutenant."

He grunted as though he'd been kicked in the belly and flashed a hand down toward his belt. He carried his gun on the left side, in front, with the butt pointing to the right. It makes for a nice fast draw, but there's no percentage in pulling a gun when another one's looking right at you.

I said: "Why don't you?"

He said: "Uh . . . Mullaney! You startled me for a second."

I said: "Didn't you expect me, Lieutenant?"

"Why should I?"

"You didn't think I'd let a man of mine get shot down without doing something about it, did you?"

"Say, that was shame. I knew who he was, of

course, the minute he was brought in. But I
didn't give your pitch away. He's down on the
books as unidentified right now."

I said: "Swede Olson had been working for me
for five years. The best man I had. We lived in the
same hotel—had rooms next to each other. When
we had a party we'd throw them together."

"It's certainly a shame, Mullaney. Anybody in
this business takes his chances. He's gambling
with his life every time he makes a move."

"You've lost your gamble, Lieutenant."

He went for his gun then and fast, and I let him
slide it clear before I touched off my own. I wasn't
more than five feet from him, and in the dusk the
orange flashes from the gun seemed to reach right
out to him. He started to fall with the first but I
put two more on top of it for good measure. And
went around the corner of the house just as the
back door opened and Mrs. Down started letting
off steam.

I was out of the alley that ran back of Down's
garage and on a cross street before I met anybody,
and by that time all anybody could see was a
tired-looking fat man, going along about his
business.

Torrey's work habits don't sound especially efficient, nor
his life-style conducive to clear thinking, yet he managed to
turn out an impressive number of good stories during the
early and middle 1940s. Steve Fisher, a colleague and
drinking companion, has left an account of a typical
evening with Torrey:

I used to write until one in the morning, or after, and so did he; and then, too often, really, I'd meet him at a bar in New York. . . . We'd drink until closing time at 4 A.M., then sometimes take a cab through the Holland Tunnel to New Jersey where the bars remained open until 6.

As for how Torrey did his work:

Roger met one of those lady authors at a meeting of the American Fiction Guild. A pert little blonde. I'll call her "H," which is close enough.

That was the day love came into Roger Torrey's life. She moved into the hotel room with him.

They both liked to drink, but liquor is expensive, so Roger made a rule. His writing table was on one side of the room, her desk on the other. Each would sit in front of his/her typewriter, their backs to one another, and the one to finish his/her story first could then have a drink. The other would have to wait until her story was completed. I say "her" in this case because H couldn't write as fast as Roger, and he, that bastard, would sit there on the floor boozing it up and taunting poor "Mommy."

According to Fisher, the couple eventually left New York for Florida:

Roger and H reached Florida all right, and sending their stories on to New York, earned enough to live on—and booze on. They were happy, H told me. Perhaps Roger Torrey's first and only happiness.

Then one afternoon he felt poorly and lay down on a couch and asked if she'd make him some tea. H brought the tea. Roger sipped it, thanking her, then rested his head on the pillow.

"Hold my hand, Mommy, because I'm going to die."

She held his hand and Roger Torrey closed his eyes for the last time.

Morton Wolson told me recently that he had intended to hold on to his real name and reserve it for the serious literary work he meant someday to do. So when he started writing for the pulps in 1939, he used the pen name Peter Paige. His first sales were made to Fanny Ellsworth, and when Ken White took over at *Black Mask*, Wolson sold to him there and at *Dime Detective*. His most popular character was Cash Wale—described in a blurb as "the pint-size private peep"—who usually appeared in *Dime Detective*. Wolson was fond of White, but not the story ideas he'd now and then come up with:

One time when we were having lunch at Bruno's Pen & Pencil . . . and I was about a week shy of entering World War II, he suggested I have Cash Wale overhear some G.I.'s plotting a crime and enlisting in the Army to go after them! I guess, to paraphrase G.B.S., those who can, write—those who can't, edit. Also, on that occasion, Ken inadvertently introduced me to Martinis. He downed three dry ones before lunch and, like the bumptuous young idiot I was, I followed suit. Following the lunch, I went to see my then agent, Sidney Sanders' office on Fifth Avenue, where, talking to one of his assistants I became nauseous, asked for the men's room key, managed the two long corridors to the indicated door, got the key in the lock—and awoke on the floor.

In the mid-1940s Ray Bradbury sold stories to such pulps as *Detective Tales*, *New Detective*, and *Dime Mystery*. Bradbury has said that writing science fiction and horror for the pulps was relatively easy. But "the detective tales, because they required hard thinking, prevented my flow, damaged my ability to use my intuition to the full. They were, as a result, quite often, walking wounded."

While the pulps continued to showcase private eyes throughout the decade—from Richard Deming's Manny Moon to William Campbell Gault's Mortimer Jones—they made room for an increasing number of writers, such as Bradbury and Brown, who avoided such traditional heroes. Another such was John D. MacDonald, who became one of the most successful of postwar pulp writers. He said,

I wrote stories in such dogged quantity that often, when I had more than one in a magazine, the second had to be published under a house name. . . . In 1946 I tried to keep at least thirty stories in the mail at all times. When I finished a story, I would make a list of the magazines which might be interested and then send it out again and again until it either sold or the list was exhausted. There were lots of magazines then. There were lots of markets then. There were lots of readers. Bless them!

What MacDonald was doing in many of his pulp stories was warming up for the crime novels—*The Brass Cupcake*, *The Damned*, etc.—that he'd write when he moved into paperbacks in the following decade. He was a transition figure and we can move from him to the last go-round of the pulpwoods.

Chapter 13

Dead and Done For

In the autumn of 1950 you could have walked up to almost any newsstand in the country and bought the latest issues of *Dime Detective*, *Black Mask*, *Detective Tales*, *Hollywood Detective*, and *Popular Detective*. Just three years later every one of those titles was dead and gone, along with most other pulps, detective and otherwise. In this final chapter we'll take a look at what happened and what caused it.

Essentially the history of the popular arts can be seen as a history of one format supplanting another: pulps taking over from dime novels and fiction weeklies, talkies replacing silent movies, LPs easing out 78s. Pulp magazines were done in by two of the most formidable mass-entertainment innovations of the twentieth century—the paperback book and television.

The paperback offered about the same amount of reading material as an average pulp for the only slightly higher price of twenty-five cents. The most serious thing the paperback did was encroach on the pulp outlets. To buy a

hardcover book you had to go to a bookstore or a department store—or, for some of the cheaper hardcover reprints
in large drugstores—paperbacks invaded the newsstand
and were usually displayed right alongside pulps, comics,
and movie magazines. In their early days they specialized
in category fiction, just like the pulps, with the largest
number of titles being in the mystery and detective field.

Pocket Books pretty much began the paperback boom in
1939. It issued thirty-four reprints that year, of which four
were mysteries. Fifty-three reprint titles followed in 1940
and nineteen of those were mysteries. Originally Pocket
Books favored mostly sedate and traditional mystery writers such as Agatha Christie, Ellery Queen, Carter Dickson,
and Dorothy L. Sayers. But as the forties progressed, the
company added an increasing number of titles by Erle
Stanley Gardner, Dashiell Hammett, and Raymond
Chandler. Avon jumped on the bandwagon in 1941,
producing twelve two-bit reprints that year. Half of them
were mysteries.

Popular Library was founded in 1943 by Ned Pines and
Leo Margulies, longtime partners in the Thrilling line of
pulps. They reprinted nearly seventy titles during their
first three years, every single one a mystery. Among the
writers on the Popular list were Leslie Charteris, John
Rhode, Rufus King, Nicholas Blake, Craig Rice, and
Anthony Boucher. Dell went into paperbacks in 1943 also,
and nearly all of its first three dozen titles were mysteries
by the likes of Rex Stout, Geoffrey Homes, George
Harmon Coxe, and Ellery Queen. Bantam entered the
field in 1945, publishing reprints of Frank Gruber, Eliza-
beth Daly, Leslie Ford, and Geoffrey Household among its
early books.

A great many lesser paperback outfits came and went in the forties, such as Bonded Mysteries, Handi-Books, Green Dragon, Red Arrow, and Hangman's House. These outfits concentrated on mysteries, including some originals, by Cleve F. Adams, Hilary Waugh, Ken Crossen, and Norbert Davis.

The Signet colophon first appeared on paperbacks in 1948. That same year Signet reprinted Mickey Spillane's *I, the Jury*. The novel introduced Mike Hammer, a tough private eye who Spillane has admitted was influenced by Race Williams. The twenty-five-cent edition went on to sell several million copies, something no hard-boiled detective pulp had ever done. And it dealt with sex more openly than any of the pulps dared. Subsequent Hammer reprints also sold in the millions.

Fawcett dealt another blow to the pulps when, in 1950, it introduced its Gold Medal line. What Gold Medal specialized in was original novels. Some were merely sleazy, but others were in a tough, hard-boiled style that seemed somehow more knowing and more contemporary than that of the surviving pulps. Early Gold Medal authors included John D. MacDonald, Charles Williams, and Richard S. Prather.

The other prime suspect in the killing of the pulpwoods was television. Still considered a novelty at the end of World War II, television sets were to be found in only 1 percent of American homes. By 1953, however, 50 percent of the homes in the country had sets, and at the end of the decade, when the figure had jumped to 90 percent, a good deal of everybody's leisure time was being taken up with viewing and not with reading. In addition to such pioneers as Milton Berle, Ted Mack, and Arthur Godfrey, private detectives and cops began to grace the television screen. *Martin Kane, Private Eye* first aired in 1949, followed by *Rocky King, Inside Detective* in 1950, *Mark Saber* in 1951, and *Dragnet* in 1952.

Sales figures on many of the detective pulps had begun to decline in the postwar forties. The increasing competition from paperbacks and television didn't help. Street & Smith, sensing the end before most of their competition, closed down their pulp operations in the summer of 1949, killing off *Detective Story, Love Story, Doc Savage,* and *The Shadow*—every title except *Astounding.* In the same year A. A. Wyn shut down *10-Story Detective* and *Ten Detective Aces.* Three years later he started Ace Books, Inc. The earliest paperbacks were Ace Doubles, offering two novels back-to-back. Two Doubles came out each month, one featuring mysteries and the other westerns. Wyn had come up with a new way to package material similar to what he'd been selling in his pulps.

The final issue of *Black Mask* was dated July 1951. For its last few issues the venerable pulp had tried another sprucing up. Trimmed pages returned, illustrations were dropped, each story carried a short introduction in the *Ellery Queen's Mystery Magazine* manner. These issues were smaller than pulps in their dimensions, though larger than digests. Popular Publications now abandoned the long-held policy of using only first-run material. At least half of each issue was made up of reprints from various titles. Brand-new stories by Robert C. Dennis and Richard Deming rubbed shoulders with old yarns by Raoul Whitfield, Cornell Woolrich, and George Harmon Coxe. In the very last issue there was a new G. T. Fleming-Roberts short novel as well as one of Richard Sale's Daffy Dill tales from *DFW* and a 1927 Harley Quin episode by Agatha Christie. An attempt was made by another publisher to revive the magazine in 1974. Only one issue, made up entirely of reprints, came forth. For all practical purposes *Black Mask* died in 1951.

DFW made a brief comeback in 1951 under the title of *Detective Fiction*. It survived for seven monthly issues. The format was identical to that of the slicked-up *Black Mask* and there was the same blend of old and new—John D. MacDonald and Robert Turner side by side with Whitfield and Woolrich. *Detective Tales* and *New Detective* also spent their final days looking like their sister publications.

Dime Detective had stopped living up to its name back in the summer of 1944, when its price was boosted to fifteen cents. There was a hike to twenty-five cents in the spring of 1950. From 1951 the magazine was a bimonthly, but unlike many of the other Popular periodicals, it retained its pulp format to the end and there were no reprints. The final issue was dated August 1953 and included stories by Stewart Sterling, Robert Turner, and Richard Deming. Deming's Manny Moon has the distinction of being the last series private eye to appear in *Dime Detective*. Many of the people who made their living from the detective pulps didn't suspect they'd fold as soon and as suddenly as they did. Richard Deming, for instance, once told me,

> I did not see the complete end of the pulps coming as quickly as it did, and neither did most of the editors in the field. Although all of us could see them dying. In 1950 I decided to try full-time writing. At the time I was living about 500 miles

from New York City. I had my agent arrange me
interviews with a half dozen of the pulp editors to
whom I had been regularly selling and went to
New York for a few days. I came away with
sufficient assignments to bring me an estimated
$800 a month just from pulp writing—not a bad
income at the time. On November 1, 1950, I
resigned my job. On November 7 Harry Widmer,
then editor of *Black Mask* plus a few others, was
fired. . . . By the end of November every editor
I had talked to in New York was out of a
job. . . . I made $1,200 during the next twelve
months.

Deming went on to become a prolific mystery novelist in
the paperback field.

Fifteen Detective Stories was launched with an August
1953 cover date, apparently intended as the successor to
New Detective. Larger in size, it resembled a true-
detective magazine rather than a pulp. Even thus dis-
guised, and featuring such authors as William Campbell
Gault and Walt Sheldon, the title failed to thrive. By the
spring of 1955, after but a dozen issues, it, too, was gone.

What replaced the pulps, for a time, anyway, were the
digest-format magazines. Digest-size publications were
nothing new. The diminutive *Reader's Digest* had been
around since 1922, and in the 1930s several other midget
magazines showed up on the stands. Street & Smith tried a
digest-size detective magazine called *Hardboiled* in 1936,
and in 1930 Gilbert Patten (who, as Burt L. Standish,
wrote all the Frank Merriwell novels) had published a

small pulp titled *The Pocket Magazine*. Neither of these succeeded. *Ellery Queen's Mystery Magazine* was introduced in 1941 by the publisher of *The American Mercury*, which was also being issued in digest size. Publishers of the 1940s seemed a bit more taken with the format and several digests resulted. *Rex Stout's Mystery Magazine*, *The Saint's Choice*, *Craig Rice Crime Digest*, and *Avon Detective Mysteries*, like *EQMM*, filled their pages chiefly with reprints. Unlike *EQMM*, none of them was a hit.

Things changed in the fifties. While the pulps were closing down, new detective digests were being started. For the most part this new batch avoided reprints. *Manhunt, Pursuit, Verdict*, and *The Saint Detective Magazine* came in 1953. *Alfred Hitchock's Mystery Magazine* began in 1956, and several lesser titles followed throughout the rest of the decade.

Mike Shayne Mystery Magazine, which also made its debut in 1956, was probably the closest thing to a pint-sized pulp. Published by pulpwood veteran Leo Margulies, in its early years the magazine featured stories by the likes of William Campbell Gault, Hal Ellson, W. T. Ballard, Richard Deming, William R. Cox, Frederick Nebel, and Cornell Woolrich.

Manhunt, published by Michael St. John, was one of the most impressive of the digests and one of the sturdiest. It went through 113 issues before shutting down in 1967. A sort of slick pulp, the magazine offered hard-boiled fiction by such authors as Mickey Spillane, Evan Hunter, Bruno Fischer, William P. McGivern, David Goodis, Frank Kane, and the ubiquitous Richard Deming. "It was the most vital force in the mystery and crime field at the peak of its success," Deming once said. "And historically is probably as important as the old *Black Mask*." Several mainstream writers, among them Erskine Caldwell, James M. Cain, and Nelson Algren, were on the contributors' list as well. Undoubtedly the best-known private eye to appear in the magazine was Ross Macdonald's Lew Archer, seen in five short stories in the first two years of publication.

By the late 1960s all but the hardiest digests—*Queen, Hitchcock, Shayne*—were gone. The pulps themselves have remained dead. Over the years relatively few of the thousands of private-eye stories that appeared from the 1920s to the 1950s have been reprinted, or for that matter even preserved. Frederic Dannay began a modest salvage operation in the 1940s, while the pulpwoods still flourished, by reprinting some *Black Mask* and *Detective Fiction Weekly* stories in *Ellery Queen's Mystery Magazine*, and he rescued nearly all of Hammett's pulp short stories and novelets, gathering them together in a series of paperback collections. More recently anthologies of pulp detective stories have been put together by myself, Bill Pronzini, and William F. Nolan. Small presses have issued collections of the work of such writers as Fredric Brown, W. T. Ballard, and the incomparable Robert Leslie Bellem. There is still, however, a great deal of first-rate material that is simply lost and gone.

Bibliography

Books

Allen, Dick, and David Chacko. *Detective Fiction: Crime and Compromise*. Harcourt Brace Jovanovich, 1974.

Anderson, LaVere. *Allan Pinkerton: First Private Eye*. Dell Yearling, 1972.

Bacon, Daisy. *Love Story Editor*. Gemini Books, 1966.

Baird, Newton. *A Key to Fredric Brown's Wonderland*. Talisman, 1981.

Baker, Robert A., and Michael T. Nietzel. *Private Eyes: 101 Knights*. Popular Press, 1985.

Barreaux, Adolphe. *What a Gal! Sally the Sleuth*. Wings of the World Press, 1986.

Bellem, Robert Leslie. *Dan Turner, Hollywood Detective*, ed. John Wooley. Popular Press, 1983.

———. *Spicy Detective Encores*. Winds of the World Press, 1986.

Bendiner, Robert. *Just Around the Corner*. Dutton, 1968.

Boucher, Anthony. *Multiplying Villainies*. A Bouchercon Book, 1973.

Bradbury, Ray. *A Memory of Murder*. Dell, 1984.

Brown, Fredric. *Before She Kills*. Dennis McMillan, 1984.

———. *The Freak Show Murders*. Dennis McMillan, 1985.

———. *Homicide Sanitarium*. Dennis McMillan, 1984.

———. *Mostly Murder*. Pennant, 1954.

———. *Thirty Corpses Every Thursday*. Dennis McMillan, 1965.

Carter, Nicholas. (Richard Wormser). *Death Has Green Eyes*. Vital, 1946.

———. *Park Avenue Murder*. Vital, 1946.

Chandler, Raymond. *Pick-up on Noon Street*. Pocket Books, 1956.

———. *The Raymond Chandler Omnibus*. Knopf, 1964.

———. *Selected Letters of Raymond Chandler*, ed. Frank MacShane. Columbia University Press, 1981.

———. *The Simple Art of Murder*. Pocket Books, 1964.

———. *Trouble Is My Business*. Ballantine, 1984.

Cini, Zelda, and Bob Crane. *Hollywood: Land and Legend*. Arlington House, 1980.

Cook, Michael L. *Monthly Murders*. Greenwood, 1982.

———. *Mystery, Detective and Espionage Magazines*. Greenwood, 1983.

Cowley, Malcolm. *A Second Flowering*. Viking Press, 1973.

Davis, Frederick C. *The Moon Man*. Pulp Classics, 1974.

Drew, Bernard, ed. *The Hard-boiled Dames*. St. Martin's, 1986.

Durham, Philip. *Down These Mean Streets a Man Must Go*. University of North Carolina Press, 1963.

Everson, William K. *The Detective in Film*. Citadel Press, 1972.

Finch, Christopher, and Linda Rosenkrantz. *Gone Holly-wood*. Doubleday, 1979.

Fugate, Francis L., and Roberta B. Fugate. *Secrets of the World's Best-selling Writer* [Erle Stanley Gardner]. Morrow, 1980.

Geherin, David. *The American Private Eye*. Ungar, 1985.

Goodstone, Tony, ed. *The Pulps*. Chelsea House, 1970.

Goulart, Ron. *Cheap Thrills*. Arlington House, 1972.

————. *Line Up Tough Guys*. Sherbourne Press, 1966.

————, ed. *The Hardboiled Dicks*. Sherbourne Press, 1965.

Gruber, Frank. *The Pulp Jungle*. Sherbourne Press, 1967.

Hackett, Alice Payne. *70 Years of Best Sellers*. Bowker, 1967.

Hagemann, E. R. *A Comprehensive Index to Black Mask*. Popular Press, 1982.

Haining, Peter. *The Art of Mystery & Detective Stories*. Chartwell Books, 1986.

Hammett, Dashiell. *The Big Knockover*. Random House, 1966.

————. *The Continental Op*. Vintage Books, 1975.

————. *The Creeping Siamese*. Dell, 1951.

————. *The Maltese Falcon*. Modern Library, 1934.

Haycraft, Howard. *The Art of the Mystery Story*. Simon & Schuster, 1946.

Hoppenstand, Gary, and Ray B. Browne. *The Defective Detective in the Pulps*. Popular Press, 1983.

Hoppenstand, Gary, Garyn G. Roberts, and Ray B. Browne. *More Tales of the Defective Detective in the Pulps*. Popular Press, 1985.

Hubin, Allen J. *The Bibliography of Crime Fiction: 1749–1975*. Publisher's Inc., 1979.

Hughes, Dorothy B. *Erle Stanley Gardner: The Case of the Real Perry Mason.* Morrow, 1978.

Jones, Robert Kenneth. *The Shudder Pulps.* Fax, 1975.

Lamparski, Richard. *Lamparski's Hidden Hollywood.* Fireside, 1981.

Lavine, Sigmund A. *Allan Pinkerton.* Dodd, Mead, 1963.

Layman, Richard. *Shadow Man* [Dashiell Hammett]. Harvest/HBJ, 1984.

Macgowan, Kenneth. *Behind the Screen.* Delta, 1965.

Madden, David. *Tough Guy Writers of the Thirties.* Southern Illinois University Press, 1968.

McKinstry, Lohr, and Robert Weinberg. *The Hero-Pulp Index.* Weinberg, 1970.

Murray, Will. *The Duende History of the Shadow Magazine.* Odyssey, 1980.

Nebel, Frederick. *Six Deadly Dames.* Gregg, 1980.

Noel, Mary. *Villains Galore.* Macmillan, 1954.

Nolan, William F. *The Black Mask Boys.* Mysterious Press, 1987.

———. *Dashiell Hammett: A Casebook.* McNally & Loftin, 1969.

———. Dashiell Hammett: A Life at the Edge. Congdon & Weed, 1983.

Parish, James Robert, and William T. Leonard. *Hollywood Players: The Thirties.* Arlington House, 1976.

Pronzini, Bill, ed. *The Arbor House Treasury of Detective & Mystery Stories from the Great Pulps.* Arbor House, 1983.

Reilly, John M. *Twentieth Century Crime and Mystery Writers.* St. Martin's, 1980.

Roberts, Garyn G., ed. *A Cent a Story! The Best from Ten Detective Aces.* Popular Press, 1986.

Roddick, Nick. *A New Deal in Entertainment: Warner Brothers in the 1930s*. BFI Books, 1983.

Ruhm, Herbert. *The Hardboiled Detective*. Vintage, 1977.

Sampson, Robert. *Yesterday's Faces*, Vol. 1. Popular Press, 1983.

———. *Yesterday's Faces*, Vol. 2. Popular Press, 1984.

Schatz, Thomas. *Hollywood Genres*. Temple, 1981.

Schreuders, Piet. *Paperbacks, U.S.A.* Blue Dolphin, 1981.

Schwartz, Nancy Lynn. *The Hollywood Writers' Wars*. Knopf, 1982.

Shaw, Joseph T. *The Hard-boiled Omnibus*. Simon and Schuster, 1946.

Slung, Michele B., ed. *Crime on Her Mind*. Pantheon, 1975.

Smith, Henry Nash. *Virgin Land*. Vintage, 1957.

Steinbrunner, Chris, and Otto Penzler. *Encyclopedia of Mystery & Detection*. McGraw-Hill, 1976.

Thorpe, Edward. *Chandlertown*. St. Martin's, 1983.

Traylor, James. L. *Dime Detective Index*. Collectable Books, 1986.

Turner, E. S. *Boys Will Be Boys*, Michael Joseph, 1957.

Tuska, Jon. *The Detective in Hollywood*. Doubleday, 1978.

Whitfield, Raoul. *Death in a Bowl*. Quill, 1985.

Woolrich, Cornell. *Nightwebs*, ed. Francis M. Nevins, Jr. Harper & Row, 1971.

Zinman, David. *Saturday Afternoon at the Bijou*. Arlington House, 1973.

Articles

Barson, Michael. "'There's No Sex in Crime': The Two-fisted Homilies of Race Williams." *Clues: A Journal of Detection*, Fall/Winter 1981.

Cox, J. Randolph. "The Dime Novel Detective and His Elusive Trail." *Dime Novel Roundup*, December 1985.

———. "More Mystery for a Dime." *Clues*, Fall/Winter 1981.

———. "Nick Carter, Fact or Fiction." *Dime Novel Round-up*, June 1985.

———. "The Pulp Career of Nicholas Carter." *Xenophile*, March–April 1976.

Drew, Bernard. "Hoh-Hoh to Satan: *Detective Fiction Weekly's* Nutty Series Heroes of the 1930s." *Clues*, Fall/Winter 1981.

Fisher, Steve. "Pulp Literature" [Roger Torrey]. *The Armchair Detective*, January 1972.

Gardner, Erle Stanley. "Getting Away With Murder." *Atlantic Monthly*, January 1965.

———. "Lester Leith, Impersonator." *Ellery Queen's Mystery Magazine*, Introductory Notes, May 1950.

———. "Speed Dash." *Atlantic Monthly*, June 1965.

Goulart, Ron. "The Pulpwood Private Eyes." *The Comics Buyer's Guide*, September 28, 1984.

Gruber, Frank. "Lester Dent." *The Armchair Detective*, July 1969.

Layman, Richard. "The Changing Face of Crime Fiction: *The Black Mask*." *AB Bookman's Weekly*, May 5, 1986.

Lewis, Dave. "The Backbone of *Black Mask* [Frederick Nebel]. *Clues*, Fall/Winter 1981.

Mertz, Stephen. "The Further Adventures of Robert Leslie Bellem." *Xenophile*, March–April 1978.

Murray, Will. "The Ancestors of Batman" [*The Black Bat*]. *The Comics Buyer's Guide*, October 7, 1983.

———. "An Informal History of the Spicy Pulps." *Risque Stories*, March 1984.

———. "Lester Dent." *Clues*, Fall/Winter 1981.

Nevins, Francis M., Harold Knott, and William Thailing. "Cornell Woolrich: A Bibliography." *The Armchair Detective*, July 1969.

Nevins, Francis M. "The World of Cleve F. Adams." *The Armchair Detective*, May 1975.

Nolan, William F. "The Crime/Suspense Fiction of Ray Bradbury: A Listing." *The Armchair Detective*, April 1971.

"Raymond Chandler's Los Angeles." *L.A. Style*, Special Anniversary Issue, June 1986.

See, Carolyn. "The Hollywood Novel." *Tough Guy Writers of the Thirties*. Southern Illinois University Press, 1968.

Tonik, Albert. "John Nanovic: Editor." *The Pulp Collector*, Fall 1985.

Traylor, James L. "Tod Ballard: An Appreciation." Introduction to W. T. Ballard, *Hollywood Troubleshooter*. Popular Press, 1985.

INDEX